"Simone's inspiring story of overcoming the odds to become the first Jamaican and first Caribbean WNBA player will pull at your heart strings. It's a story of resilience and triumph that must be told."
The Hon. Olivia Grange, CD, MP, Minister of Culture, Gender, Entertainment and Sport of Jamaica

"As the first Caribbean and first Jamaican WNBA player, Simone was one of the pied pipers of the league. A player that inspired others, brought smiles to their faces and authentically connected with the fans. Her rise to become one of the elite athletes of the world, is truly a story of perseverance, belief and adaptability. Her story is one that will inspire all who read it to reach for the stars and believe."
Donna Orender, Former WNBA President

"Simone Edwards has been one of the Seattle Storm's biggest cornerstones. She has been an integral part of the Storm's success both on the court and in making our mark in Seattle's community. I am so thankful to have had the opportunity to be a part of her journey by working with Simone and winning a Championship. She is even more incredible knowing this inspirational story."
Anne Donovan, Former Seattle Storm WNBA Head Coach

"As a Jamaican American, Simone held high the torch for women and basketball players around the world representing herself with the kind of quiet leadership and humility that draw people to her. Her memoir is an inspiration to anyone who has a calling on his/her life to leave the world in a better place than they found it."
The Hon. Dr. Geneive Brown Metzger, Former Consul General of Jamaica (New York)

UNSTOPPABLE

To: Dave

I hope you will enjoy reading about my journey.

Sending love and peace your way.

Love

Simmey Edwards

UNSTOPPABLE

A MEMOIR OF ADVERSITY, PERSEVERANCE & TRIUMPH

SIMONE EDWARDS
with JOBI TYSON

The details and conversations in the book, all come from the author's recollections, though they are not written to represent word-for-word transcripts. Rather, the author has retold them in a way that evokes the feeling and meaning of what was said and in all instances, the essence of the dialogue is accurate. Some names and identifying details have been changed to protect the privacy of individuals.

ISBN: 978-0-9989697-0-1

10 9 8 7 6 5 4 3 2 0 6 0 7 1 7

Printed in the United States of America

∞This paper meets the requirements of ANSI/NISO Z39.48-1992 (Permanence of Paper)

I dedicate this book to all underrepresented children with big dreams.

My deepest gratitude to my mother Beryl Edwards, and Nancy "Mama" Coley for the foundation you gave me and for your dedication, hard work, unconditional love and support. Because of you two strong women, I was able to withstand every obstacle and found strength through adversity.

And finally, in loving memory of my dear brother Gary and precious sister Cassandra, with love.

CONTENTS

Foreword by NBA Legend Dikembe Mutombo xi

Special Note by Coach C. Vivian Stringer xiii

Introduction xv

Chapter 1: Sweet Home Kingston 1

Chapter 2: You Are Special 13

Chapter 3: Beating The Odds 23

Chapter 4: Kill Mi Wid It 35

Chapter 5: She's Got Next 41

Chapter 6: Chasing The American Dream 49

Chapter 7: Hawkeye Nation 67

Chapter 8: No Pain, No Gain 75

Chapter 9: Put Me In Coach 85

Chapter 10: When Preparation Meets Opportunity 95

Chapter 11: Fruits Of My Labor 105

Chapter 12: A Star Is Born 113

Chapter 13: Rise Of The Jamaican Hurricane 121

Chapter 14: Once A Champion, Always A Champion 139

Epilogue 151

Acknowledgments 155

About the Authors 159

FOREWORD
BY DIKEMBE MUTOMBO

Readers of this memoir about Simone "Jamaican Hurricane" Edwards are in for a rare treat. The hero's journey is always an important tale to tell – over and over. As a one-time foreign professional basketball player in America, I can relate to Simone's journey so well, and her achievements represent a triumphant ending for the underdog.

Tough beginnings in a gang-infested, poor village. Confusion about what to do and why and how to do it. Intense isolation. Determination in the face of seemingly insurmountable obstacles. Scarred and weary, the hero, standing atop a distant hill, emerges victorious. Simone is that hero, and her journey serves to inspire, motivate and help others navigate their own "hero's journey."

Through motivating speeches she gives around the globe, Simone makes her unusual story accessible to those who doubt their own capabilities because of so many barriers that seem stacked against them. She candidly recounts the pain and struggle of growing up in immense poverty and the importance of discovery, hard work and, at times, luck to her personal and professional success. She credits her mother, coaches and earth angels who believed in her when those with power seemed to doubt her, count her out or want to see her fail. The Jamaican Hurricane rose above every obstacle, purposeful and persevering through it all, and finally emerging as living proof that every champion was once a contender who refused to give up.

Simone's unique journey touches myriad social issues – from gender, to class, to race, to ethnicity – and how she was able to beat the odds on the road to her ultimate success. Her incredible story resonates on many levels and shines a light on the sport of women's professional basketball as she spells out in detail how she maintained resilience in the face of opposition. The journey you're about to take as you read the almost unbelievable tale of Simone Edwards is a reflection of hope in the face of inconceivable obstacles. The power in this book will change your life, confirming that your current circumstances do not dictate your future.

DIKEMBE MUTOMBO
NBA Hall of Famer
Chairman & President, Dikembe Mutombo Foundation

A SPECIAL NOTE FROM
HALL OF FAME COACH C. VIVIAN STRINGER

Simone is a true inspiration to all young people. She has never looked for reasons why she could not do something or achieve a goal. She continues to strive and to make a difference for herself and for others. I remember Simone as a bright-eyed young lady who had a burning desire in her heart to be the best that she could be with all endeavors.

It was clear to me early on as Simone's head basketball coach at the University of Iowa from 1993 to 1995, that Simone's drive was different than most. She was highly motivated, willing to work harder on a regular basis than many of her peers. Simone's eyes would light up at the prospect of learning something new or different.

Take for instance when in various "line-ups" to do warm-up or teaching drills, most of her teammates would stand passively awaiting their turn to perform. Simone, I promise you, would wisely use the waiting time as an opportunity to create and rehearse the motor sequence in her mind to optimize learning and her execution success. Simone was also a great student. She was someone who truly appreciated and capitalized on the opportunity to receive higher education. Her mindset is one that truly believes: "It doesn't matter where you've come from but where you are going."

When considering the many individuals that I have had an opportunity to technically train as a basketball coach, Simone Edwards was a standout. She began a career in basketball without having had any formal training or real success as a basketball player before high school, but went on following college Division I play to become a professional basketball player and champion for the WNBA Seattle Storm in Seattle, Washington.

Knowing Simone since her college days, she has continued to manufacture pathways for herself despite having "less than" most as a child. She is a visionary and a living inspiration to everyone because of her uplifting spirit and because she has accomplished so much having come from a place of minimal resources and opportunities.

In her years at The University of Iowa, there was no question in my mind that she would be outstanding in the years ahead. Why? Because she refuses to say "no." She refuses to make any excuse for herself. She is always going to find a way to get it done. It doesn't surprise me, therefore, that she has written this memoir. Simone's inspiring story of beating the odds through extraordinary life circumstances is one of the strongest sports memoirs in recent years.

Love,
COACH C. VIVIAN STRINGER

INTRODUCTION

When I was a child, I couldn't see beyond the poverty that surrounded me until I learned how to read. In books, I discovered that there was a big world out there and that happy endings were possible. My belief in happy endings came from my love of fairy tales, which were my escape into a world of hope and dreams. Still, for much of my childhood, I thought you needed to start with money to achieve your goals or become successful. Not many of the poor people around me overcame their financial circumstances, or gave me examples of what I could aspire to be.

One thing I did know was that my mother was a strong woman who worked all day to keep us clothed and fed. My inspiration came from seeing my mother work through sickness and health. She did it, so why shouldn't I? I also knew that I needed money for college, and that was where I would get the education to become successful to be able to give back to the people I loved and who had supported me. I had no idea that opportunities would present themselves to me even though I grew up in the ghetto.

I read books to take me to places I'd never been and to live vicariously through other people's experiences. I chose to write this book so I could touch other lives the way many books have touched mine. This is my way of spreading hope, inspiration and motivation to people who need encouragement. I want anyone who feels as if they are stuck in their present situation to know that it's only temporary and the universe has so much more to offer despite their current circumstances.

As a young person, I saw a bleak future ahead of me and felt as if my life could have ended at 17, right after high school. My story will take you through my journey of perseverance and triumph over bullying, sexism, classism, and abuse among other obstacles. Despite a tough beginning, I decided to create my own path and made up my mind that I would never quit, no matter how hard the journey. I knew it started with believing in myself, because many others were going to doubt me. Doubt they did, but it didn't stop me. I cried, I prayed and I cursed. Whatever it took to keep me going, I dug deep and found it. I had only one choice, and that was to succeed. I left myself with no other options. Failure wasn't an option. My journey was tough, but I survived it. So can you.

They say, "If you believe it, then you can achieve it," but I realized success is more than believing. It's about envisioning yourself as successful in every situation and setting goals, which are not based solely on your ability to set them but even more so on your ability to achieve them. In order to achieve your goals, you first have to set them based on your gifts and abilities.

I had an extraordinary vision of who I could be. As a child, I saw myself as a champion. I went from running barefoot in school track races to becoming the first Caribbean and first Jamaican WNBA player, but the journey in between is what I hope will motivate you to become the best possible you, just as I did. Despite how poor I was, my dreams and goals were always free, so I set them and used determination, hard work, effort, commitment and self-love to achieve them. My path may not be yours to walk, but I hope it will help and inspire you as you travel yours.

CHAPTER 1

SWEET HOME KINGSTON

I awoke in the middle of the night to the sound of gunshots. I felt in my gut that someone I knew was killed. I tried counting the gunshots. Maybe six rounds. After the gunshots ceased, I peeked out the window with mommy, clinging to her gown. Neighbors peeked out their doors, one by one. It was 1977, and at 4 years old, I knew from experience to wait until I heard that first scream to know exactly where the shooting took place. It didn't take long before police gathered around the crime scene. On the pitch-black road, neighbors held homemade kerosene lamps – glass bottles with rolled up soaked paper pushed in the bottles to create a torch for light. Some neighbors were falling to the ground in sorrow, while others chattered about who they thought the shooters were. I was saddened as I overheard loved ones of the deceased crying at the top of their lungs while screaming, "You murderers!" All too often, the sound of gunshots filled the night air, which was usually gang wars. At night the gunmen moved about, wearing army-style clothes, the same way our military soldiers dressed. The only way we could tell they weren't real soldiers was to glance at their feet to see if they were wearing old, worn shoes.

I lived in Gold Smith Villa, which we called Angola or Gola. Gola was a small impoverished village in Kingston, Jamaica. Our village was almost hidden, given the way you had to walk through other communities to find it. It was nicknamed Angola from its comparison to the bloody Angolan Civil War, involving thousands of deaths, since Gola was one of the most feared village because of our gunmen. Yet, oddly in the midst of this tension, conflict and gang violence, I was not afraid to move about the village and surrounding areas, in part because this was my norm. As dangerous as the gangs were, oddly enough, we found some comfort in knowing that the gang leader, which we called our area leader, protected our village. While we and our neighbors slept, they stayed up all night on watch. Still, there were more and more killings. Sometimes, killings ceased for a while once the gangs agreed to some sort of peace offering. But not for long, causing chaos in the midst of paradise.

In Gola, there were gang wars with adjoining communities and at each entry and exit point, we had to cross the gully – a long ditch cut into the soil formed by running water – over a bridge to enter nearby villages, Hermitage and Manley Avenue. The tension of ongoing battles made life hard. As a child, I despised the area leaders. Their lifespans were short, but as soon as one of them was killed, another area leader, maybe even worse, took charge. They were either killed by police, a rival gang member or one of their own members, leaving several children fatherless. Sometimes, an area leader would take over neighbors' homes, using guns to force them out, with nowhere to go. Their presence caused destruction in too many lives. Mommy always said, "If you live by the gun, you die by the gun." That may be true in most cases, but then there were the innocent bystanders who were just victims of circumstances.

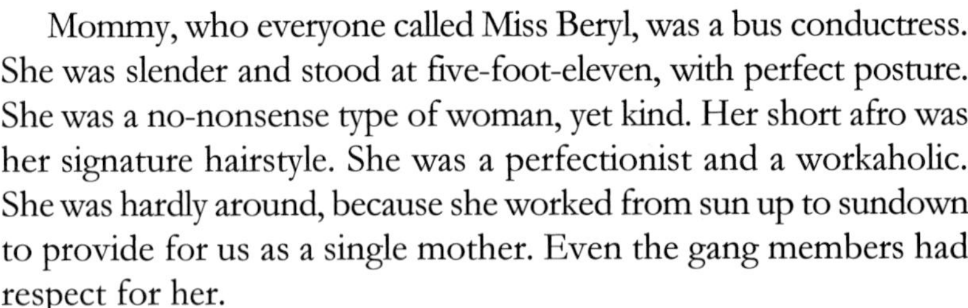

Mommy, who everyone called Miss Beryl, was a bus conductress. She was slender and stood at five-foot-eleven, with perfect posture. She was a no-nonsense type of woman, yet kind. Her short afro was her signature hairstyle. She was a perfectionist and a workaholic. She was hardly around, because she worked from sun up to sundown to provide for us as a single mother. Even the gang members had respect for her.

I shared a room with my three older brothers, 6 year old Gary, 12 year old Steve and 13 year old Junior. I shared a twin bed with Gary, while Junior and Steve shared a queen bed. I felt safe sleeping in the same room with my big brothers, since I was afraid of the dark and with all the violence that was happening outside.

Our little house had two bedrooms and a two-burner stove with no kitchen sink. There wasn't one yard in Gola without fruit trees, including ours. Our yard had trees filled with mangoes, plums, bananas, cherries, and limes, while the neighbor's plentiful grapefruit tree hung over our yard.

Our village had a public bathroom with showers and toilets, since most neighbors could not afford them in their homes. Before mommy was able to add a bathroom with a shower and toilet, we had an outhouse in our backyard. Although we had a bathroom, if the water pressure was low, we had to fetch water at the public restroom three houses down. The public restroom reeked of urine, and huge ugly toads sat around the entrance and inside the shower stalls. There were about five shower stalls, and the lines were always long. Neighbors often fought over whom would be next in line.

Most times, we cooked, ironed, washed and cleaned without electricity or water. We had a coal iron to press our clothes, using coals or wood to make a fire, then we'd place the iron on top of it until it got really hot. Next, we wiped the bottom of the iron with a damp cloth and placed a cloth over our clothes before we pressed them. If the gas stove fizzled before mommy was done cooking, she continued cooking on the coal or wood. We kept the coal and wood in an old hubcap. If we ran out of coal, we went searching for dry wood to make a fire. We had to make do with what we had.

Every morning our alarm clock was the cock-a-doodle-doo of our neighbor's rooster. Promptly at 4:30 a.m. each work day, the bus company's staff bus picked up mommy. Her best friend, Nancy Coley, whom I affectionately called Mama, would sometimes stay over at our house on weekdays to get me ready for school. Mama Nancy was a petite five-foot-three woman with soft, gray hair that she wore in two plats. She lived in a neighboring village called Hermitage. From the time I was a newborn, Mama Nancy cared for me as if I was her own child. She helped mommy so much by keeping watch over my brothers and me while mommy worked.

She gave me the same loving attention and protection that she gave her own daughters, 11 year old Cassandra, 13 year old Maxine, 20 year old Marcia, and 22 year old Pam, all of whom were like blood sisters to me.

On mornings, before school, Mama Nancy and I walked about two miles up the dirt roads, to her house to pick up her tray and stool, as well as assorted candies, fruits, and biscuits that she sold on the side of the road another mile away. Most of the walk was in darkness, as there were only a few scattered light poles along the route. Since I was afraid of the dark, Mama Nancy held my hand tightly, giving me a sense of safety.

When the sun finally peeked out, she started selling her candies, fruits and biscuits. I enjoyed sitting next to her, learning the ropes. She'd give me a piece of candy or a biscuit as I watched people and cars pass by, until it was time for the bus to depart for school.

At St. Francis All-Age School, I quickly noticed – as many of my classmates did – that I was considerably taller than other students my age. At recess, while playing with my friends, I fell onto the pavement and split my chin. Blood soaked into the ground. Some older boys laughed and shouted, "Her feet too big. She tripped on her feet." Until that moment, I had no idea my feet were big, compared to children my age. But, like the rest of me, my feet were growing fast. I embarrassingly ran to the school nurse, who put iodine on my chin, which turned by chin orange. After I walked out her office, the same bullies then chanted, "Goldie chin!" The nickname lasted for weeks. To avoid their taunts, I hid from them during breaks. I soon came to feel a bit overwhelmed by the constant bullying, merely because I was different. Because of my height and lankiness, I didn't fit in, which gave bullies the license to taunt and terrorize me. I couldn't quite grasp the troubling environment I was facing at school.

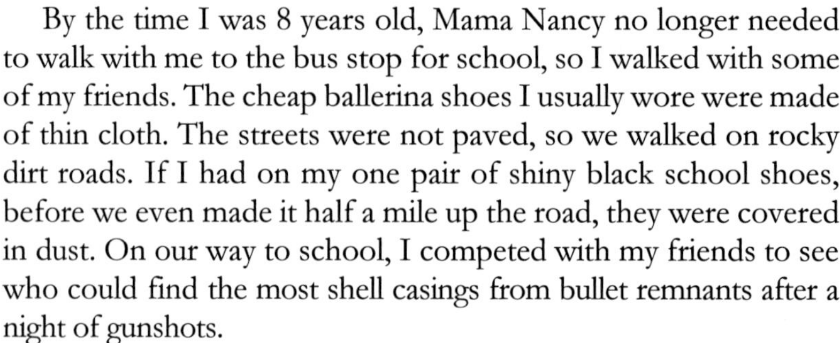

By the time I was 8 years old, Mama Nancy no longer needed to walk with me to the bus stop for school, so I walked with some of my friends. The cheap ballerina shoes I usually wore were made of thin cloth. The streets were not paved, so we walked on rocky dirt roads. If I had on my one pair of shiny black school shoes, before we even made it half a mile up the road, they were covered in dust. On our way to school, I competed with my friends to see who could find the most shell casings from bullet remnants after a night of gunshots.

Mommy provided for the four of us children as best she could. Despite what we might have needed or wanted, we had to do with what she could afford. I often had to wait for months until she could scrape together enough money to buy me another pair of shoes. There was much discomfort walking on those dirt roads with the rocks piercing the bottoms of my feet through those ballerina shoes. It was as if I was walking barefoot, which most times I did. My toes filled the shoes all the way to the tip until my big toe pushed through.

As mommy began to realize I was growing faster than the typical grade-school child, she started buying shoes one size larger. I stuffed those shoes with tissue, adjusting the amount of tissue as I grew into them. Just when I thought there was nothing worse than the discomfort of ballerina shoes, mommy bought me plastic shoes. With the plastic shoes, if I stood in the sun too long, the shoes felt like I was getting second-degree burns on my feet. Living in Kingston, I was in the sun year-round, so I couldn't escape the sweltering heat and the way those shoes melted onto my feet. Most of the children in my village were poor, so walking barefoot was normal. I knew mommy was saving up for a durable pair of walking shoes for me, so I tried to patiently deal with the daily torment.

Amidst all this craziness of a gang-infested village wrapped in poverty, Gola was so full of life, dreams and drama. As poor as I was and as dangerous as our village could be, I always found myself laughing and being entertained. I often climbed the mango tree in our front yard to watch people fighting or cursing at each other. I learned rhythm and how to dance, since there was always music playing at our next-door neighbor's house, and on weekends, he would put up his big speakers and let the music blare out into the road. Neighbors danced for hours in the road to the pulsing, pounding rhythms. I wasn't allowed to go onto the road while mommy sold desserts and juices at home on weekends, so I stayed in the front yard and danced by myself.

The neighbor directly behind our house was a Rastafarian who smoked Ganja all day. The strong scented smoke swept through our yard with great frequency. With that daily contact, I never felt the need to try Ganja, since I had inhaled enough second-hand smoke.

I got excited whenever a water shortage affected our village, because I knew I could leave the house to fetch water with my friends. We never knew when low water pressure would completely shut off our water supply. The route I had to take first required that I cross a field to get to the mile-long route of dirt roads that took me to the water source. I walked barefoot in the scalding sun, and all too often would get pieces of glass caught in my feet on the hot, weary journey. After a while, my feet became used to the pain of constantly hitting my toes on rocks, crossing fields and going through paths of bushes to fetch water.

I became very familiar with the route to a house owned by a Rastafarian everyone knew as Dred, and I used his water pipe to fill my large water jug. Dred was a farmer who owned a well, and he was kind enough to let people fetch water from his house for free.

One day, I prepared to go back home, I situated the jug of water on my head. Mama Nancy taught me how to use tree branches as padding on my head to keep the large water jug from falling off. I took breaks along the way picking mangoes on nearby trees to rest and relieve my hunger. When I returned home, I emptied the water into a plastic barrel in the backyard. Mommy had gone to the market, and my brothers were not home.

Minutes later, the front door flew open. A tall, stout man, dressed all in black crept into my house. Although he was a family friend, I flinched. There was just something about the way he looked at me whenever he was around that spooked me. His appearance frightened me with his scary beast-like features.

Our house was on a corner lot, set well back from the road, and in our small village, there was seemingly never a need to lock our doors. Unlike killings, break-ins rarely happened because we had so little to steal. If someone did break into a home, the thief was severely beaten by the gang members. I wasn't sure why *The Beast* was inside my house. "Where is your madda and braddahs?" he asked, as he moved closer towards me. "Mommy is not here, but my brothers are coming back soon," I said, knowing that I had no idea where my brothers were at that moment. "It's OK, I came to speak with your madda. I'll wait here for her," he said, as he plopped down on a chair. I tried to convince him that mommy wouldn't be home anytime soon because she left not so long ago. I was saying all of these things expecting him to leave, but it only motivated him to stay. I felt deep down inside like there was something wrong, since I'd never been alone in his presence.

"Here's some money. Go get us two sodas," he said, handing me several coins to go across the road to the neighbor's shop. I thought this was a good way to go find my brothers outside, even though I didn't feel comfortable leaving him in my house alone. I ran outside, anxiously looking for my brothers, but none of them were in sight. *The Beast* wasn't even from our village, and I had never been alone with him. Where could my brothers be?

I returned to the house, handed him his soda and placed mine inside the fridge even though I wanted to drink it. "It's hot out there, girl. Drink your soda," he said, now blocking the door. I felt more uncomfortable, so I told him I was going to go find my brothers, hoping he would leave. When I tried to go around him to exit the door, he grabbed my wrist and said, "You can't leave until you touch it." At first, I had no idea what he was talking about, but that naivety didn't last long. With his free hand, he unzipped his pants and pulled out his penis. I began to sob. Then, he tightened his grip on my wrist, insisting that if I didn't touch his penis I couldn't leave. "I am going to tell my daddy! He is a policeman, and my mommy will be mad and never let you back in her house," I screamed as loud as I could as I tried to twist my wrist from his grip. He was massaging his penis in his one hand, and with his other hand, he tried to force my hand to touch it.

I cried even harder, and he yelled, "Shut up! You too stupid and ugly. It's not going to hurt you! Just touch it and stop acting so foolish." My mind was racing, as I tried to think of a way to escape. "I am going to tell!" I screamed out as I hit his hand. He got angry and he twisted my wrist so hard I thought it was broken.

"I will touch it, just let my hand go," I said.

"Just do like I am doing," he said, as he released my hand. "If yuh tell yuh madda, she won't believe yuh and will beat yuh for lying because I will tell her yuh lying and yuh just a little pickney, so she will believe me," he said in Patois, hoping to frighten me.

He succeeded quite well in frightening me. "Okay I will touch it, but I need ice for my wrist because you broke it," I responded, holding my wrist and acting as if it was in more pain than it actually was. "Yuh don't need nuh ice," he said, as he released my wrist to pull his pants down to expose himself fully. I knew that was my moment to run.

There were three exits in our house – the front door that he was blocking, the door that led into mommy's room, and the back door near the kitchen, which was a few feet away from where I was standing, which opened directly out into our backyard.

I made a dash for that back door, and he made a vain effort to catch me, doing the best he could with his pants down around his ankles. I was simply too fast for a man running with his pants down. I started running to Mama Nancy's house. As I ran across the bridge, I spotted my brothers in the gully catching fish. I said nothing to my missing protectors. I reached her front yard out of breath but relieved. Once inside her house, I said nothing to Mama Nancy about what had happened, even though I knew she would believe me. I wanted what had happened earlier inside my house to just disappear. Later, Mama Nancy walked me back home believing the story I had told her – that my brothers were gone, and I was afraid to stay alone at the house.

When we arrived, mommy and my brothers were home. I was too afraid to tell anyone about my frightening encounter with *The Beast.* I had already been taught about inappropriate touching, by mommy and Mama Nancy, however nothing prepared me for what had happened. Mommy taught me a lot about life, truth and skills needed. I did my best to listen and learn. That experience with *The Beast* made it clear that mommy and Mama Nancy were warning me and teaching me for a reason. I didn't tell Mama Nancy what had happened with *The Beast* since I was afraid if I had, he might attack her and, unlike mommy, who kept a machete under her pillow, Mama Nancy couldn't fight back. I kept it to myself thinking the problem was mine, and just couldn't conjure up the courage to talk about *The Beast.*

From time to time, I'd see *The Beast* lurking around in Gola, but I kept my distance as he'd give me this leering, warning stare. I disconnected myself from reality, and held this awful secret which haunted me. My heart never got past that stolen innocence.

I learned how to climb trees from watching my brothers and through my own trial and error. I also learned to accurately throw heavy stones that, from a good distance, could knock mangoes out of trees. This skill allowed me to create my own hustle, like Mama Nancy, collecting and selling mangoes. I was able to expand my hustle beyond mangoes to include plums and guineps – small sweet grape-like fruit with green skin. Next door to Mama Nancy's house was a big guinep tree. I'd climb to the rooftop to pick guineps, then sell all my fruits to people walking by on the street.

Mama Nancy let me sell my fruits next to her, and soon she opened a bank account for me. I was so excited because she said if I kept saving, I'd be able to buy that red Volvo in which I dreamt of driving her and mommy. In the quest to save even more money, I had to accumulate more fruits to sell. It was always a great feeling, the cool breeze caressing my face as I stood underneath a big mango tree eating a mango that had fallen off, with or without my help. At times, my first cousin Keisha and friend Deshi would join me on my adventures, climbing the forbidden tree, on university grounds. On one particular day, we strayed onto the university campus to raid its flourishing mango trees.

When I couldn't knock any more mangoes off while standing on the ground, I climbed up the tree. Keisha and Deshi watched for the security guards as I was in the tree. I felt a strong gust of wind and held on tightly to the firmest tree branch in order not to fall. I was worried as the wind rocked me back and forth. I tried my best not to fall and hurt myself.

"Simone, him a come!" Keisha shouted in Patois, waving her hand to signal to me to come down while Deshi quickly gathered up all the mangoes in a bag. I saw the security guard walking towards us and shouting at us to leave. I quickly hurried down the tree, getting a few scratches along the way. We ran until he was out of sight. I had the bag of mangoes and made sure not even one fell out. I could feel the sweat running down my face and burning my eyes. We sold the mangoes on the side of the road, and anticipated sharing what was leftover – enjoying the "liberated" fruit.

One evening, I was supposed to be leaving Mama Nancy's house to get home before dark. Instead I stopped at her next-door neighbor's house to play with friends, and darkness crept up on me. I got scared because I knew I needed to be home before dark, so I went back to Mama Nancy's house. She agreed to walk with me down the road. I suddenly jumped in fear as a loud gunshot echoed across the road, but Mama Nancy didn't budge. She calmly said, "It's a firecracker", but I knew better.

It was dark, and hardly anyone was on the road. As we reached the top of the entrance that led to Gola, the bus came to a stop near us. Mama Nancy waited to see if anyone getting off the bus was going to Gola so I could walk with them, since it was a mile away. She recognized a man we knew from my village who got off the bus and asked him to take me to my house.

In order to get to my village, I had to walk down a hill that had no light except the stars beaming light our way. The path was bushy and rocky and had a gutter made of cement and blocks that led from the top of the gully. The track was narrow, and we had to cross over the gully with a small wooden bridge and a dirt field. I thought of the gunshot earlier and just wanted to get home. There were never gunshots without one or more dead bodies afterwards. We started walking down the path, which was filled with holes caused by heavy rains, so I stayed close to the man every step of the way.

Suddenly, I heard a rustling noise behind us. I turned around and saw six gunmen rushing out of the bushes. My heart was beating so hard I thought it would burst through my chest. I grabbed the man's hand tightly and whispered to him, "They are going to kill us. Let's pray."

He agreed, but I didn't hear him praying. He probably was scared, too. The gunmen then disappeared into the dark. The man said, "They are our guys, so they won't hurt us." Before he could mutter another word, I just took off, darting across the fields so fast I didn't even feel the ground under my feet.

When I got home, mommy wasn't home yet. I was deeply concerned that about her safety since she had to walk home along that same path. I told Gary what had just happened and suggested we set out to meet mommy when the bus came, as we could hear her bus and know when she was near. As afraid as we were, we went to the lit part of the field to wait for her bus to arrive.

Soon, we saw mommy walking across the field, then we ran to meet her. I told her I heard a gunshot and passed gunmen, and she said she saw someone lying in the gutter near the start of the hill but didn't think much of it because people loitered there sometimes, and when they were drunk, sprawled most anywhere. The next morning, a dead body was found in that gully.

It wasn't paradise everywhere on the island. But, this was my life of Gola.

CHAPTER 2

YOU ARE SPECIAL

Mommy was so strict that I feared her more than I feared feathers. I have no idea why I was terrified of feathers. Perhaps, in my past life I endured a traumatic experience with chicken attacks or something. With that being said, fear of feathers didn't hold a candle to mommy's wrath, or her death stare, in which she didn't have to say one word. She'd just give me 'that look,' and I immediately stopped in my tracks, even if that meant halting my escape from feathers.

I was 10 years old and still wasn't allowed to play on the road with my friends. So, one day I conjured up a plan to escape the front yard, in which I just knew I could get mommy to agree. On this Saturday, there was a church group that visited our village to preach the gospel. We were familiar with this church group, as they occasionally had church service that usually lasted a couple of hours. And, as a devout Christian, I presumed that mommy would gladly permit me to attend the church service, while she was staying home to sell desserts and juices. And, I was right.

As I closed our zinc gate behind me, I smirked, since I had just outsmarted mommy. I was certain that my plan was air-tight. I ran to my friends, who were congregated by the small gathering of people singing gospel songs and praising God. Then, one of my friends mentioned that there was a free karate movie showing at the community center, which was a short, two-minute walk. I was so excited because karate movies were my favorite. I was certain that I was a kung-fu master in my previous life – as all those movements just felt natural to me. I calculated how long the movie would be, so I could watch the movie and then return to the church service before everyone had left. I had it all planned out. I was free as a bird, clapping and singing a gospel song as my friends and I trekked to the community center. When we arrived, all the seats were filled, resulting in us standing to watch Jackie Chan in *The Drunken Master*. And I enjoyed every minute of it.

When the movie ended, I stepped outside of the community center, and realized that it had gotten darker much quicker than I'd expected. Even worse, I didn't hear the church group anymore. I ran over to see if anyone was still there, but everyone was gone. Of all the times to shorten their church service, they chose this evening? Either way, on the dark road, only God could have helped me then.

I stood in front of my gate at home, regretting my decision, with my heart beating louder than a drum. At that moment, I would rather have run through a field of one-hundred feathers than experience the wrath of mommy. I tried hard to go unnoticed, but my effort was all in vain as the old rusty gate creaked louder and louder as I slithered in my slender body. "Jesus, have mercy on me, please. I will never lie to mommy again if you tell her not to punish me," I fearfully prayed. Although, He was probably totally disgusted with this wayward child for lying then skipping His holy service to watch Jackie Chan. I closed the gate behind me, then tiptoed to the front door, as if I was walking on egg shells. I hoped mommy had fallen asleep without realizing that I wasn't home. I attempted to open the door, but it was locked. So, I quickly crept around to the back door, turned the knob silently, but it was also locked.

At this time, I began reciting all the verses in the Bible that I knew by heart, which was only two, so I kept repeating those two verses over and over again. I made all kinds of deals with God, offering to give up sugar cane, fruits, beef patties and even karate movies in order not to be punished.

In a final attempt, I tried opening the back windows, since Junior sometimes left them open for a cool night breeze. It was just my luck that on this night, all of the windows were locked. So, I lightly knocked on the room window, hoping my brothers would hear me. Then Junior finally came to the window and peered out, disclosing that mommy instructed them not to open the door for me. At this instance, I made another deal with God to offer Junior as a human sacrifice. After all, he was the firstborn.

I knew then that I'd soon meet my Savior.

I broke one of mommy's main rules, which was to be inside the house before dark. I paced outside the house as if I was a prowler. Then, I panicked as I wondered where the heck was mommy. I know she knew that I was outside. It was like she was intentionally making me sweat. It was torture not knowing what was going to happen when I entered the house.

I was pacing back and forth on the front porch, and five minutes might have passed, when the front door flung open. It was mommy who gave me the death stare as she stood in her night gown with one hand behind her back. And, I assumed it was not the Bible she was hiding back there. She said calmly in that knowing voice, "Where have you been? Church was over hours ago." I paused and stuttered, trying to come up with a lie, but I was so frightened of what was hiding behind her back, I just started crying. Tears, intended to help my dire situation, were merely wishful thinking. Mommy just stood there, waiting for an answer.

I kept my distance while still remaining close enough to keep my eyes on what was lurking behind her back. "I was watching a kung-fu movie," I contritely admitted. She just kept staring at me like I was a puzzle she was trying to solve. Then, she started moving toward me. With no time to spare, I made a desperate plea for God to perform a miracle, since mommy always told me to "ask and it shall be given." God didn't answer, but mommy did. Revealing her belt behind her back, she said, "I allowed you to attend church service, not a movie," as she started swinging the belt. Then, my kung-fu moves kicked in as I started dodging the belt without getting hit. But, my luck was running out, because I realized that in order for me to enter the house, I probably had to surrender to a whooping. So, I blurted out, "I am sorry, mommy. I won't do it again. Pray for me, mommy. I need you to pray for me." She then looked away, and stormed inside the house. This seemed like a setup to get me inside. I wasn't falling into that trap, so I approached the door and peeped my head inside to see if she was anywhere in sight. I then tiptoed inside and softly closed the door behind me, while keeping an eye out for mommy, and her belt. I was relieved to hear mommy in her room. So, I hurried into my bedroom, slid beneath the covers, but never went to sleep. I kept getting in and out of bed to listen at mommy's door.

The next morning, I was surprised to find myself gently nudged out of my sleep by mommy. She then divulged that I was spared a whooping, because as soon as I asked her to pray for me, she couldn't keep a straight face and had to rush into her room to let out a laugh. Afterwards, she forewarned me that if I ever broke her rules again, there would be no such luck. I believed her and promised not to attempt anything like that again. Furthermore, after it was all said and done, I realized that the only miracle performed that night was the miraculous rescue from mommy's belt.

At 10 years old, despite the fact that I was nearly six-feet tall, boys were still bullying me at school. They constantly followed me around chanting in Patois, "Papaya tree, giraffe, mawga gal (skinny girl) and longy lala." When I had the courage to speak up to them, they would all charge toward me to try to fight me, but I outran them. They'd throw stones at me since they weren't fast enough to catch me. I began to realize then that I had a special gift of speed. But, I also developed a special gift of throwing stones back. I tried not to seem afraid of them, but it was one against three, and I didn't like the odds. So, I threatened them that my daddy was a police officer.

My daddy, Aston Edwards, was in fact a police officer. He was five-foot-seven, with a medium build. Daddy lived in another city several miles away, married with three children – my sisters Juddeth and Venece, and brother Wayne – and I visited with them during the holidays. He drove a black police car with tinted windows. Whenever I recognized daddy's car driving up to my school, I'd excitedly run toward his car. He made occasional visits to my school, and these visits made my day. Though, the bullies disappeared when he showed up, as soon as he left, they reappeared to taunt me.

To be teased about something I couldn't change made me feel alone, painfully different and ostracized. Unfortunately, I too, had to endure adult strangers making mean-spirited comments about my height and skinny stature, making every effort to ensure that I heard them. I was perplexed to why it was so important to them to tease me and insult me with their words. I never cried around bullies, even when the pain was overwhelming, but sometimes when I was alone, the hurt was unbearable to face, and I cried my heart out.

One Saturday morning, mommy wanted to take me shoe shopping. However, I dreaded shoe shopping, because of the shoe salesmen's shock-horror reactions to my very big feet. I was 12 years old and stood six-foot-one, wearing a size 11 shoe. Perhaps, the most discouraging was constantly hearing the words, "We don't go up to that size."

Always feeling like I stood out too much, I decided to hunch my back, assuming my height would go unnoticed. As I closed the zinc gate behind me, I hurried to catch mommy, who was speed walking to catch the bus. Once I caught up to her, she said sharply to me, "Stop hunching your back!" She directed me to correct my posture and to never hunch my back again. I revealed to her that I was teased about being tall, and she shared that she was also teased for being tall when she was my age. I never knew that.

"Don't hide who you are," she said. "Never let people make you ashamed of your height. Stand straight and be proud of your height," she continued. As we heard the bus coming around the corner, I straightened my shoulders as if I stood at attention.

Then, mommy shared three words that changed my life going forward. "You are special." Until that moment, I couldn't understand why, out of all of her children, I had to be the one who wouldn't stop growing, especially since I was the youngest and the only girl. I badly wanted to be the same height as my friends. The bullying had led me to believe that my height was an imperfection, and that the bullies' taunts were true. At least, that's what I thought until mommy uttered "You are special." Those three magical words cemented my determination to not let bullies rule my life.

I longed for my brothers to involve me, so I observed and tried to mimic everything they did to prove I was good enough to include me. But it didn't matter to them how good I got. I was always just their annoying little sister, but it broke my heart when they excluded me in their games. Though, there were times when Gary played with me, but only when Steve and Junior didn't involve him in what they were doing. When Gary and I did play together, we usually ended up arguing and fighting, but that was better than playing alone, and fighting with him made me tougher. Although we fought at times, I was confident that if bullies were around, Gary would protect me. Somehow, though, he never seemed to appear when they did, so I had to learn to handle my bully battles on my own.

As I moved through childhood, I discovered an imaginary world, becoming enthralled with fairy tale books. I learned to read at an early age, and my favorite books were fairy tales. A trash truck often discarded books at the nearby dumpster, which we called 'the Dump.' Although, I was warned to stay away from the Dump, whenever my friends and I saw the trash truck, we eagerly jumped the walls to see what books we could find in the trash. While digging through books at the dumpster, I dismissed the horrible smell and avoided the broken bottles because it felt like Christmas to be able to escape through any fairy tale books we might find. I'd climb down in the unlit furnace, which was in the middle of the Dump, to find books before they were burned. I didn't understand why people didn't give the used books to poor kids instead of discarding them, and I never knew where they came from since we didn't have a library close by. My favorite book was *Cinderella* because she was poor and struggling, and despite all her hardships, she found a way to live happily ever after. Her life sort of reminded me of mine. I could relate to the story and longed for my happy ending.

One day, I tried to outrun my friends to find books first. While alone, I stumbled on a naked man lying in the Dump, covered in books. Immediately, I called out to my friends, and we nudged him to see if he was asleep. But, he didn't move. There was a white paper taped to his face with a written message. One of the boys lifted the paper, but I turned my head, so I wouldn't recognize him. He read out the message on the paper, which said, "Informer," which was a person who snitches about criminal activities. We then hurriedly left the scene. The man's dead body scared me so much that it took me weeks to return, but I still yearned for more fairy tale books. The books were my escape from this ugly reality.

When I finally returned to the Dump, my friends yelled, "Two down here!" I thought they were joking, since we hadn't been in a while, but then I saw two more dead bodies, a woman and a man, both of whom I knew from Hermitage. That was my last straw. As much I craved fairy tales, I never returned to the Dump.

It was hard for fairy tales to grow and give hope and comfort when an ongoing horror story was wrapped around them, staining the books with ugly memories. But, just as I began feeling withdrawals from the Dump and the escape that fairy tales provided me, a library-on-wheels started coming to Hermitage, just a minute's walk from Mama Nancy's house. When the mobile library drove up, someone would yell, "The books are here!" People would run from all directions to check out books. We were able to check out the books available onboard that day to keep them for a week at a time. I was so thrilled to read more fairy tales. I was proud to have access to library books and a library card, but I still missed the unlimited book supply from the Dump, in which I didn't need a return date on my books.

I was a tough little sister who fought for inclusion and wanted my brothers to stop using my age and gender against me. Mommy shared with me that when I was younger I told her, "Men are no good. All they want to do is sit, eat and watch television while the women do all the work." I observed the men in my life and was against the seemingly different roles men and women were assigned. I thought I should be able to do and be whatever I wanted.

Hence, a tomboy and feminist was born. I grew tired of being denied the things I liked solely because I was a girl. I loved being a girl, but I disliked the roles to which I was being restricted, including the notion that girls should only play with dolls.

When I did play with dolls, I had to make my own out of paper or sticks, and they weren't very pretty. I perfected making my own toys but still wished I could have afforded the pretty dolls and fancy toys from the store.

I often asked mommy why it was frowned upon for girls to play with trucks and climb trees. I perfected climbing trees and building my own trucks, using carton boxes for the tops of the trucks and plastic bottle tops for the wheels, which I learned by watching my brothers.

Nevertheless, it was practically inevitable that I'd become a tomboy as the lone girl living amongst three brothers and hardly allowed out of our yard to go play with other girls. Mommy jokingly said she had asked God for a girl, but instead He seemingly sent her another boy. Never once did I want to be a boy, I just wanted to compete against my brothers and any other boy to prove that girls were not weak and, most important, that I was not weak.

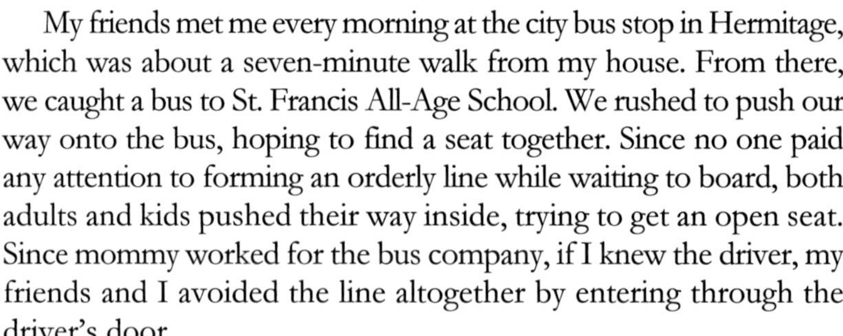

My friends met me every morning at the city bus stop in Hermitage, which was about a seven-minute walk from my house. From there, we caught a bus to St. Francis All-Age School. We rushed to push our way onto the bus, hoping to find a seat together. Since no one paid any attention to forming an orderly line while waiting to board, both adults and kids pushed their way inside, trying to get an open seat. Since mommy worked for the bus company, if I knew the driver, my friends and I avoided the line altogether by entering through the driver's door.

At school, I was usually still hungry after lunch. My belly seemed to have no bottom to it. Giving in to my hunger, I often spent my return bus fare on food sold by street vendors outside the school. As a consequence, I had to walk two hours with friends to get home, unless I noticed a familiar bus driver passing by allowing us to catch a free ride.

As we walked from school, nice cars passed by quite often. My friends and I wished our parents had those cars driving by, and we picked out the cars we wanted to have when we grew up. We made up all sorts of stories about how we managed to get them.

On our path walking home from school, there was a wealthy neighborhood that sat high on the hill, called Beverly Hills, that we passed in our parish of Saint Andrew, which stretches into the Blue Mountains. We were reminded every day as we walked from school that not everyone was poor in Jamaica.

Beverly Hills had beautiful mansions. They were like the castles I read about in my fairy tale books. They seemed to have many rooms and stairs to climb all the way to the top, unlike my two-bedroom house. They were five times as big as my house or any of the other houses in my village. As we slowly passed by, mesmerized, I'd tell my friends, "One day I will live there." They laughed in my face because we were all poor. Those wishes seemed so far-fetched. But it always brought us joy to share such fantasies together.

Beverly Hills was definitely a dream for me. It had the most beautiful scenery, with a view of the ocean from the homes. I always imagined living a great life there and having my own room. I was curious to know if their residents had a reliable water supply, never needing to leave their community to fetch water. I often wondered what it felt like being rich, never once having to worry about things like food, clothes, toys or books. And what it felt like to have pairs of shoes for everyday of the week.

As I walked past Beverly Hills every day, it appeared to be the happy ending I longed for. I pretended that I was walking home to Beverly Hills. I would walk to the top of the hill, inhale its beauty, and then walk back downhill to our difficult, impoverished reality.

Meanwhile, back in Gola, when gang wars ceased, neighbors walked the streets with empty jugs for water. Kids ran down the street barefoot. Goats wandered around. Men sat and played dominoes, some smoking Ganja. Elders people-watched, and women gossiped, as street vendors sold fruits, candies and single cigarettes. I never saw any of those occurrences, or even children playing on the streets, in Beverly Hills. It prompted me to question whether poor people had a different definition for what it meant to be rich, or maybe we just had more fun.

CHAPTER 3

BEATING THE ODDS

Mommy left the bus company to start a new career in fashion. She began sewing clothes and drapes. She was the hardest working woman I'd ever known. She had become my hero long ago. I was really happy that mommy learned how to sew because then I knew I could have trendy clothes.

She surprised me with a brand new pair of leather shoes that cost her a good penny. She explained it was better to buy quality because it lasted longer. I was so proud and delighted to not wear the cheap shoes anymore. She was proud that she could afford them.

Those leather shoes were sacred to me because once, when I was in school and in need of shoes, mommy had to give me a pair of hers to wear. I stuffed tissues into her oversized shoes and wore them every day until one day the back of the shoes split during school. I was incredibly embarrassed as I hid in the classroom, hoping none of the bullies noticed my shoe. It happened during our lunch break, when I usually went behind the building to shoot marbles with my friends. I knew they'd soon come find me and ask me to play, so I hurriedly found the arts and crafts teacher and asked for a needle and thread. I was able to hide from everybody and stitch mommy's shoes back together before my classmates noticed.

It was the last day of school for the summer break at St. Francis, and I didn't plan on returning there when classes resumed in September because I felt positive I had passed my exams to go to a high school. The Common Entrance Examinations, which are modeled on the British testing system, are taken by children, some as early as age 10, to advance into the high school system in Jamaica. Before we took the exams, we had to select the top five high schools we wanted to attend. After taking the tests, we had to wait for the results to be printed in the newspaper several weeks later.

The wait was so stressful that some students even committed suicide if they did not see their names in the newspaper, because that meant they failed and would have to stay back in school until they could take the exams again the following year. For some students, the immense pressure to pass the exams came from their parents. For others, it was the fact that a few of their friends might have passed and left them behind. Wherever the pressure came from, it was too much for some students to handle effectively. As the system was designed, it seemed to me to be far too stressful for any student to be put through.

I had failed the exam the year before because I was weak in mathematics, so my teacher and my brother Gary tutored me. I was determined to pass the second time. After the results came out, I learned I had finally passed and made it into Kingston Tech High School (KT), where my brother Gary was enrolled. I was so relieved and happy, and so were my proud parents and family. I had a good summer stretching in front of me. It made me excited to start high school.

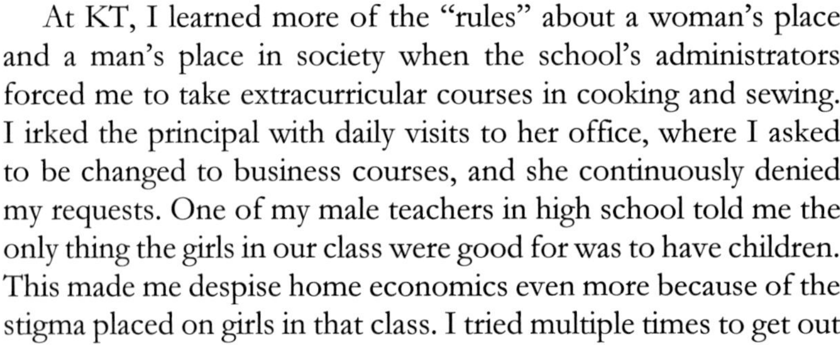

At KT, I learned more of the "rules" about a woman's place and a man's place in society when the school's administrators forced me to take extracurricular courses in cooking and sewing. I irked the principal with daily visits to her office, where I asked to be changed to business courses, and she continuously denied my requests. One of my male teachers in high school told me the only thing the girls in our class were good for was to have children. This made me despise home economics even more because of the stigma placed on girls in that class. I tried multiple times to get out of the "domestic" classes – the ones designed to mold us to fit society's perception of women.

One day, while in home economics class, one of the two male students said he no longer wanted to be in the class. He said he was getting teased on a daily basis by other boys about being in the cooking and sewing classes. As a result, the principal allowed him to change to a business class, just like that. No delay. No argument. I was so upset at her decision that I stormed into her office and told her how unfair it was. I demanded and then begged her to allow me to take business classes. Yet she was still unmoved. How dare she decide my future and who or what I was to be!

I found myself defending my stance on numerous issues while increasingly fighting for what I believed. I decided that I simply had to create my own destiny and build a new path for my future. The world around me, apart from mommy and Mama Nancy, was not giving me any of the help or support that I recognized I needed.

I didn't like sewing or cooking. I tolerated cooking because I loved eating, but it didn't factor into my future as a career. I wanted to work in the business field like my older brother, Steve. I saw that he made mommy proud, and I wanted mommy to be proud of me, too. And I wanted a path out of poverty that seemed to consume our lives.

Mommy finally went to the principal's office to ask her to change my cooking and sewing classes. The principal told her there were no spaces left in the business classes. I knew that was quite clearly not true because the business teacher had told me there were seats available and wanted to teach me if the principal agreed to it. Needless to say, I was anything but fond of my principal and her view of her female students, and it seemed as if she wasn't too fond of me either.

My maternal grandfather Willoughby James, who everyone including mommy called Uncle Willie, came to stay with us during this time. He was a pastor and a farmer back in Hanover, the parish where my mother was born. He had pretty, wavy hair, and he had the most beautiful and kind soul. But, he fell ill and, as a result, had to live with us so mommy could look after him and give him the care and love that he needed.

He was a proud and religious man and was always reading his Bible. He was the male figure in my life who made everything seem attainable. He saw the positive in everything, and I was inspired each day with him in my life.

He was slowly getting weaker and weaker and kept telling me not to worry because, when it was his time, he would be happy to see his Father in heaven.

"He doesn't need you," I argued. "I need you!"

We spent a lot of time talking about my victories in track and field competitions and the latest happenings at my school. However, he didn't talk much about himself. He just wanted to hear me talk, and I was always doing a lot of that. I liked to reminisce about spending summers in the country with him. I'd catch crawfish, and then he'd cook them for me. He'd always give me his "last penny" so that I could buy food. He was a farmer, who walked for miles with a big bag of mangoes and other foods to sell at the market. My grandfather was a big part of who I was aspiring to be. I wanted to be kind, giving, loving and, most importantly, a doctor so I could cure him. I wanted him to feel better. Why wasn't God making him better?

One day after school, I came home and ran inside to tell my grandfather how my day was and to see if he needed anything. He was not in his bed or anywhere else in the house. He was too weak to walk around so I figured mommy took him to a doctor's visit. We feared going to the doctor because, if you were poor and did not have money, you didn't receive proper care, including the necessary tests and medications. There was limited government assistance in Jamaica for poor people. I ran outside and saw Junior, who told me that Uncle Willie had been taken to the hospital and died. My heart sank. I knew Junior had a sick sense of humor, but even he wouldn't joke about something like that, would he?

Later, Gary told me that mommy had taken Uncle Willie to the hospital. "How do you know?" I asked Gary, since he had come home a few minutes after I did. He said someone who saw the ambulance told him. Mommy was at the hospital by herself, and I didn't know if I was going to see my precious grandfather again. I refused to believe he was deceased. I prayed that he was going to come back home with mommy or, at worst, be admitted to the hospital. I was a nervous wreck waiting for mommy to get home. When she finally arrived, she was alone and crying. Uncle Willie had died in the hospital.

I grieved as I experienced my first loss of someone I deeply loved. Mommy was devastated, blaming herself for something over which she had no control. She felt lost and cried out for her father. I watched her drowning in her pain as I tried to control my own so I could be strong for her. Soon neighbors and loved ones were at our house, trying to give comfort.

I no longer wanted to be home. It reminded me of him. The house smelled of him. His Bible was on his bed, so I took it, held it close to my heart and cried. God took my grandfather when I was unprepared. My grandfather was a good man who read his Bible all day long and praised his God continuously, so why didn't God heal him? I wanted to know. I could see no good reason that God took Uncle Willie from me.

Uncle Willie proclaimed that I'd be successful, and was blessed to do great things. He constantly said to "trust in the Lord" and to "walk by faith, not by sight." All those prayers I did, and yet he died without me saying a final goodbye. I was angry at God and the doctors. I was angry at being poor and too young to help. I didn't get to say goodbye. Did my grandfather know how much I loved and adored him?

I hate death.

Mommy lost her father, the man who had raised her by himself. I had never seen her this broken. I buried my pain in writing poetry. I never spoke about the loss of my grandfather at school. It was as if I was living in denial. It hurt too much, and I didn't know what to do with it.

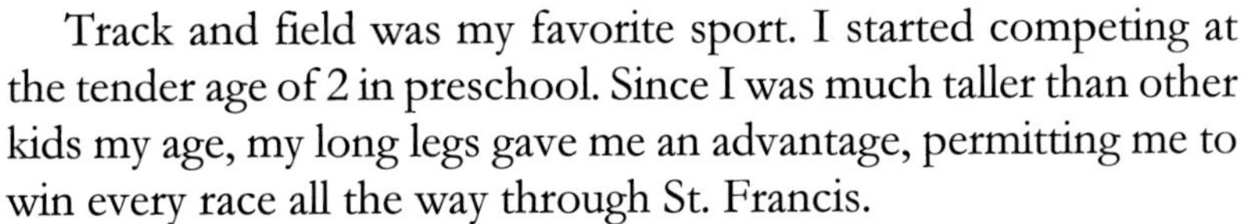

Track and field was my favorite sport. I started competing at the tender age of 2 in preschool. Since I was much taller than other kids my age, my long legs gave me an advantage, permitting me to win every race all the way through St. Francis.

Now I was hoping to find that success again in high school at KT. I knew I was good at track and field, and daddy was my biggest fan, cheering on the sidelines during every competition. Sports Day is a significant part of the Jamaican culture. Each school had its annual Sports Day, where the students were placed into different groups, separated by colors, and participated in a variety of events that tested their athletic skills. I had been a part of Sports Day since I attended St. Francis. Mommy's work schedule conflicted with my past Sport Days, but she was always so proud of me when I brought home my gold medals. I don't recall a time that daddy wasn't there.

At first at KT, I was a bit intimidated about competing on Sports Day with all the new student athletes about whom I knew little to nothing. On Sports Day, students were divided into groups, called "houses," and each house was identified by color. Each teacher was assigned a house, and my Spanish teacher, Mr. Lawrence asked me to compete for his house called "Harris," and our color was blue.

There was no real training leading up to Sports Day, but I did a lot of running with my friends in Hermitage. We always practiced competing on dirt roads in our area to see who was the fastest among us on any given day and in any given race. I won again and again.

I was signed up to run in the 50-, 100- and 200-meter races. I saw daddy and Gary standing on the sidelines before my first race, which was the 50-meters. It felt good to see them, knowing they were there rooting for me.

There were girls from the track team in that race, and they had on spikes. But I ran barefoot, since I didn't have running shoes. As soon as the starter's gun fired, I ran as if my life depended on it. Daddy had run along the sidelines during every single one of my races, shouting my name and warning me when another runner was getting too close. This made me smile and feel motivated, reminding me that he had done the same thing during all of my races at St. Francis.

My hope was to escape poverty using my gift of speed to earn a track scholarship and become a track star like so many other Jamaican runners. Despite running without shoes, I won that race and every other race that I entered that Sports Day.

I was awarded "Champion Girl," the title given to the girl winning the most points in a Sports Day competition. I had made my mark on the track field. Suddenly, the bullied girl was popular, getting a lot of compliments and congratulations.

In March 1990, in my junior year in high school, I competed for KT in the Girls Champs national track meet. All of the high schools across our island were competing for the national championship in track and field. I had been training at school, but I felt my training must be inadequate compared to the other schools' because KT had very little equipment and gear.

The national track meet was being held at the National Stadium at Independence Park, a sports and cultural complex in Kingston. Outside, the stadium was filled with the different schools' buses and their respective supporters in their school uniforms.

I didn't run hard in the first two qualifying races because they were only to qualify for the final race, which was the medal race. I was told by the coach not to use up all my energy, so I did not have to run too hard in the qualifying races. I ran just hard enough to qualify for the final race.

While waiting in the tunnel for the final race, a teammate pointed out the runners from Vere Technical High School, the most dominant school in the nation in the Girls Champs competition for years. The coach had given me some old, dirty spikes, but they didn't fit because they were one size smaller than my feet. I had trained in them once because they were given to me only a few days before the race, and my feet were in excruciating pain. I would have rather run barefoot, which was comfortable and familiar, but my coaches insisted it was mandatory to wear shoes at the national track meet.

I watched the races before mine and heard the crowd cheering for each one. People were decked out in their school's colors, and many fans were carrying flags to represent their favorite school. We didn't have many KT supporters, but I could see the faithful few yelling and anticipating each race in which a KT student would be competing.

At last, it was time for my final race. I walked out to a cheering crowd. The fans seemed overly excited about my group, I thought. Then I realized I would be competing against the national champion from the previous year in my final race.

I thought, *you got to be fricking kidding me*!

I was never one to back down from much of anything. Boy bullies? Give me a rock. Mangoes high in a tree? Keep watch. Mommy's belt look? OK, I winced! But, this was not the time to back down or fail.

I waved to the crowd as if they were cheering for me and, when my name was called, I walked to my mark. I stood up while everyone else kneeled down. I had never liked kneeling. My coach tried to teach me how to get off the blocks from that position, but I was always late. I thought the officials would allow me stand up, as I had been accustomed to, but they didn't. Not good.

My heart felt like it was beating twice as hard as I kneeled, listening for the starter's gun. In that moment, kneeling in the blocks, I shut out everyone around me and, for a second, I saw a vision of my grandfather. This was for him. But the odds were against me.

The gun went off, and all I could remember was having a late start. A few girls were already in front of me. My spikes were getting tighter and tighter on my feet. I caught up to and passed two of the runners, but it wouldn't be good enough to medal.

That was the first time I had not medaled in a race. It seemed I always won or, if I didn't win, I at least medaled. I felt as if my world had come to a crashing halt – in too-small shoes – because I couldn't run as I always had from a standing start. Thousands of spectators were watching. And the first time, daddy – my lucky charm – had missed a race, my winning streak broke. I was so crushed, as tears filled my eyes. My coach tried to encourage me. I was one of the best, too, or at least that's what I was constantly told. That's what I had believed until that moment. I always felt less than ordinary, bullied and taunted for being different. All I had ever really wanted was to be extraordinary, and running made me feel extraordinary. After that race, as far as I could see, I was no longer extraordinary. You can't be an extremely tall girl, standing at six-feet-three inches, and be ordinary. If you're as tall as I am and not extraordinary, you're someone to be mocked, taunted, teased and viewed as some sort of oddity.

I grabbed my bag after the competition and sobbed during my walk to the bus stop. On this important day, when I had hoped to win a gold medal at the national level among my peers from different technical high schools, I had failed, didn't win a medal, and was emotionally devastated.

As I was walking from the stadium, I heard someone shout out my name. I turned to see who it was. The shout belonged to a local basketball coach, Keith "Coach Smiley" Daily, who was standing with a heavyset white guy. I didn't want to talk to anyone right now and was hoping my grandfather up above had not been watching that embarrassing final race.

I recognized Coach Smiley but didn't know him personally. I had just seen him a few times when I was at the stadium. As for the heavyset white guy with him, I was sure I had never seen him before in my life. Curiously watching them approach, I was immediately conscious of how this was the first time I had ever seen or interacted with a white man face to face. I could also tell from their wristbands that both of them attended the track meet.

Great, I thought. *They saw me lose that horrible race.*

What could they possible want from me? The white guy was probably a track coach recruiting for a university in the USA. The coaches in the USA always came down to see our runners so they could offer them scholarships to run for their universities. I wanted to win solely for that reason. That was the only way I saw to get out of the ghetto.

At this point, I felt like I had let everyone down by not winning or finishing in the top three. Uncle Willie said I was going to be great because I was blessed, but all I was blessed with today was a blister from ill-fitting, old spikes and a very tender, bruised ego.

I was finally greeted by the two men, who seemed excited to see me. The heavyset white guy had a strong cowboy accent and introduced himself as Coach Gary Hudson. He shook my hand with a firm grip. I couldn't help but notice the difference in the color of our hands. His were white and pale, as if they were never exposed to the sun. He said, "I can see you're an excellent athlete!"

I was wondering if he had smoked some Ganja.

He asked me quickly and directly, "Do you want to play basketball and receive a full athletic scholarship in America?"

At this point, I was convinced someone had given him a big fat blunt! Jamaican marijuana is no joke.

In Jamaica, in my village and among the students I knew, we called America "Foreign." I dreamed about one day moving to Foreign. Coach Hudson was scouting for "extraordinary," tall girls in Kingston and heard about me.

I responded hesitantly and timidly. "I don't even know what basketball is."

Coach Smiley then introduced himself as a local women's club basketball coach and said, "I will teach you."

Then, I learned that Coach Hudson was the head women's basketball coach at the University of Oklahoma.

I was used to playing netball, a game with seven players per team that required no dribbling and allowed no running with the ball. The ball had to be passed in three seconds, but there was no backboard, and a netball was about the size of a soccer ball. I was good at it and played on the netball team for KT and for fun after school sometimes with my friends. That's where I saw Coach Smiley a couple of times when we walked to the stadium on the way home. He was on the courts next door training, but I never went over there to watch or see what game they were playing. That court had a different entrance, and the stands where people sat and watched the netball games blocked the view of the other court where Coach Smiley coached basketball.

I felt this seemingly once-in-a-lifetime offer from these men, who were complete strangers to me, had to be too good to be true. I had my guard up with these two, but I was feeling rather desperate. It was the summer leading up to my senior year, and mommy couldn't afford to send me to college. I knew that I needed some kind of change or else my future was dim, and the school principal forcing me to take cooking and sewing classes would ultimately win. Furthermore, that darn sewing needle stuck me too many times. It was as if I was stitching my fingers, not the darn material to make some clothes.

It felt like this was God's way of answering my prayers after all those days of walking, crying, and praying to Him, as I had been taught to do. Mommy, Mama Nancy, and Uncle Willie told me that God always heard my prayers. The timing couldn't have been better, even though I didn't know what I was getting myself into.

Right then and there, I accepted the basketball training offered by Coach Smiley.

When I reached home, mommy was in the kitchen. "I met two coaches today, and one had a funny accent like the cowboys on TV, and he offered me a basketball scholarship," I told her. "I can go to a university in Foreign."

She looked puzzled, as if she was skeptical of the news. "What's basketball?" she asked.

I replied, "I have no idea."

CHAPTER 4

KILL MI WID IT

On that first Saturday, my first practice with Coach Smiley, I showed up 15 minutes late. I had run two hours from home in 100-degree sweltering heat, and he was extremely upset that I was late. I only scraped up enough for one-way bus fare, which I wanted to use on my way back home, so I ran to practice in my attempt to get there on time. I didn't want to bother mommy for money. As a single mother, she wanted to give us more and was already doing as much as she could. So, I left as early as I thought I needed to get there on time.

I found out as I got closer that I hadn't left early enough.

My clothes were drenched in sweat, and I was exhausted, hungry and dehydrated. Coach Smiley did not take kindly to any of his players being late. When he asked me why I was late, I stood in silence and said nothing.

Coming from a family with few resources, I was tired of how poverty interfered with everyday life. I was being offered a life-changing opportunity, and I had to make small decisions about things like bus fare because I didn't want mommy to feel bad or use money for me that should have been spent on basic necessities.

I figured I'd be tired after practice and would want a ride home. I didn't want mommy to carry more weight on her shoulders to help me reach my dreams. I grew tired of being a burden to the sole provider in the family because I knew she was working so hard to provide for us. People sensed that I was poor, but they didn't know exactly how poor I was and how that impacted everything I tried to do or wanted to do. Being poor, people treated me differently. Consequently, when I wasn't with other people who were as poor as I was, I tried to hide the severity of my poverty. I had been bullied because of being poor. I didn't trust the world enough to let people know how poor we were. So, I often did what I could to hide how being so poor was impacting my life.

When Coach Smiley asked about my tardiness, I responded with silence because of my vulnerability. I didn't want him to know about my desperation or how I'd run most of the way. Not knowing what was really happening, what could he think other than he had a cocky, tall athlete in front of him who didn't want to admit her laziness or guilt? Unaware of my real effort to be there on time, he got so upset that he decided to teach me a lesson.

Coach Smiley had me hold two large stones in each hand and perform a defensive stance, which involved me crouching in a squatting position and sliding side to side, without my feet crossing each other, outside on the paved ground. My first day of training didn't involve any ball work. Instead, he had me do intense coordination work, including squats, slides, and pivots along the lines while he sat in the shade and shouted instructions at me. Yet, I didn't complain or explain to him about my two-hour trek. I just did as instructed. And through his efforts to punish me, to assert his authority and demand respect, I practiced on the scorching ground barefoot.

When a few onlookers asked Coach Smiley to ease up on me, he walked over to me to end the punishment. Defensive, angry, determined and prideful, I shouted at him, "Kill mi wid it."

As if these dreadful drills weren't punishment enough, two of his female players showed up and decided to add fuel to this first day's stressful fire, shouting to Coach Smiley that my movements were awkward and that I could never learn the game. They said he was wasting his time with me. Their cruel words recharged me, and I took my anger and pain and turned them into drive. I was determined to show them and Coach Smiley that I was chosen for a reason. I wasn't going to let this opportunity pass me by. He ordered them to leave, and they finally did.

When this first intense training day ended, I hobbled off the court and across the street to the "Sky Juice Man," Mr. Riley, where I used my bus fare to buy a sky juice – a mixture of scraped ice, syrup and water in a clear plastic bag, with a straw in it. I walked back to the court and handed it to Coach Smiley. He was surprised I'd bought him a sky juice after the agonizing first practice, but that was my way of extending an olive branch because this experience was my way out the ghetto that was Gola. As hard as practice was, I understood he expected discipline and he really wanted me to succeed. That first practice wasn't going to break me.

I was relieved when he offered me a ride home because I had used my bus fare and didn't have the strength to walk home. During the ride, I told myself that if this is basketball, I had to be mentally and physically tough. There was no way I was going to let this opportunity pass me by.

It was all so exciting, to the point of being a bit overwhelming. I was also thinking this was too good to be true; to be presented with an opportunity like this was so surreal. It seemed impossible for a poor girl from a small village to be offered a scholarship to a major American university, an opportunity made even more unreal because it was offered for the very reason I was bullied my entire childhood and adolescence – my exceptional height. I didn't even know the game, but Coach Smiley convinced me that it wasn't a fairy tale.

This opportunity was real.

After my first practice, I was never late again and never missed a practice. I took the bus to the stadium, and if Coach Smiley couldn't take me home after practice, I walked, which was tough because I was hungry, tired and worn out, but I could always count on a mango or plum tree on the way to quench my hunger. My long walks after practice were filled with tears at times because I felt like I was too far behind in learning the game of basketball. How could I ever catch up to the other athletes, who had played the game so much longer and made it look so easy? How am I supposed to run full speed down a court while dribbling a basketball when I can hardly walk a straight line?

As I walked, I thought about mommy and Mama Nancy and how much they sacrificed, and it helped me refocus my motivation. I felt empowered again. Those two women were definitely my inspiration. I wanted to be one of the ones who made it out the ghetto, so I could come back home and make a difference for children going through the things I knew too well as a result of grinding, violent poverty. I just had to make this little sacrifice as I walked two hours home from practice on a far-too-regular basis.

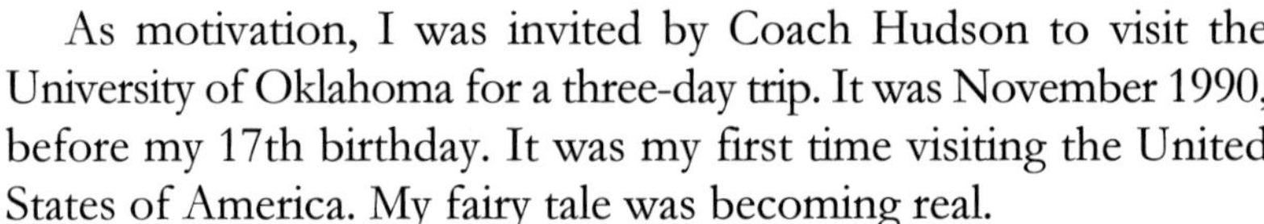

As motivation, I was invited by Coach Hudson to visit the University of Oklahoma for a three-day trip. It was November 1990, before my 17th birthday. It was my first time visiting the United States of America. My fairy tale was becoming real.

To this point, I had a very simple picture of "Foreign" that had been shaped by watching American shows, like cowboys and Indians, and *The Abbott and Costello Show*. Those programs and commercials were the extent of what I thought I could expect in Foreign.

I sat on the plane feeling so accomplished. I was going to visit a university in Foreign. The feeling was dreamlike.

I landed in Oklahoma City, about 20 miles from the campus in Norman, and waited for my suitcase at baggage claim. There were people passing by and speaking with that funny accent, just like in the movies I had watched about the cowboys. I looked around for Coach Hudson but didn't see him anywhere. After a bit, I decided to go outside to see what America looked like.

It was the middle of winter in Oklahoma. As the terminal doors opened, a cold breeze hit me. I felt as if it entered my body, froze my bones and exited through my back. A lady standing next to me told me it was "only 50 degrees" outside. She seemed unbothered by the cold. I guess she was used to freezing temperatures. My body was in shock. I screamed at the top of my lungs, ran back inside the airport and retrieved my suitcase. I'd never experienced anything this cold before. I went to a restroom and put on extra clothing that was packed away inside my suitcase. Coming from year-round warm temperatures in Jamaica, I wondered how people could live and function in this type of weather. Not even my fridge at home got that cold!

I went back to the lobby and waited. Shortly after, one of the university basketball players, Dana Posey, picked me up. She was the sweetest person and was my host for the weekend. On our drive to the university, she asked about my trip and told me a little about her experience as a player at the university. I didn't dare complain about my bone-chilling cold experience. She took me to her apartment, where I would stay throughout my trip. I thought it was so remarkable that she had her own apartment. I had always dreamt about having my own room, but I couldn't imagine having my own apartment.

After I unpacked, we went to the university's gym, where Coach Hudson greeted me. I walked inside in awe. It was my first time ever seeing a wooden basketball floor. It was the most beautiful indoor gym I had ever seen. I was used to playing outside in the hot sun on concrete courts. This was definitely some kind of dream. How else can you explain beautiful, shiny, wood floors on which to play basketball?

The women basketball players all came to the gym to greet me. They were wearing sweatshirts and sweatpants with their team's name and logo on them. I admired their shoes and couldn't wait to join the team so I also could have all that cool gear. We exchanged questions about warm-and-sunny Jamaica and freezing-cold Oklahoma. They laughed at me for saying it was freezing. A few said they couldn't see themselves leaving Jamaica for Oklahoma. I guess it's different from the outside looking in. I didn't want to leave my beautiful country, but my opportunities were extremely limited there because of poverty.

I was introduced to other people on campus. I even met the university athletic director as we toured the athletic department. All the players had just finished their workouts for the day and left for classes or their campus residences. Dana took me on a campus tour, which included attending a class with her to see what it was like. The classroom had over 300 students.

Afterwards, I headed out to my first dinner in America with Dana and Coach Hudson. I ordered steak, which I'd never had before. Coach Hudson assured me that I could order anything I wanted, and since I had a whole lot of backed-up wants, I added the grilled shrimp. We spoke about their training system and how the team was doing, and he asked me about how my training with Coach Smiley was progressing in Jamaica. I told him it would be better if the sun wasn't always kicking my butt.

After dinner, I was too tired and cold to do anything else, so Dana took me back to her apartment. A full tummy and a warm blanket was enough for me to pass out for the night.

The next day, I got to experience my first college football game. I mostly stared at the players' uniforms because I understood nothing about the game, except that there were a bunch of guys smashing into each other. That, I didn't mind watching. The atmosphere at the football game was amazing, with the schooner wagon and matching white ponies making their way across Owen Field in a triumphant victory lap after every OU score. This was the first I'd ever seen or heard anything about schooners. The bands were playing as if attempting to outdo each other. The cheerleaders were flipping in the air and motivating the large stadium crowd. In awe, I watched the crowd, which I was told was over 70,000 people, as they did the wave and shouted, cursed, and screamed throughout the game. I sat there, wishing my family and friends could be here to share this amazing, unreal experience with me.

CHAPTER 5

SHE'S GOT NEXT

After coming down from Cloud Nine following my visit to the University of Oklahoma, I was even more determined to succeed and work extra hard. I felt that visit was meant for Coach Hudson to impress and motivate me, and it worked. I craved the opportunity even more, although I was told that what I had experienced as bone-chilling cold was very mild compared to the approaching winter temperatures.

It was my high school senior year and, as much as I tried to concentrate at school, all that dominated my mind each day was everything Coach Smiley had taught me the day before. I couldn't afford my own basketball to train with, so I trained in my mind by going over practice moves Coach Smiley taught me and performing physical training with an imaginary basketball.

Again and again, we repeated the same drills. The daily training was intense and physically demanding. I was easily drained of moisture and energy as I worked out in the direct sun, heat, and high humidity. But I knew that I didn't have long to prove myself. My skills were nowhere close to where they should be at this level of basketball. I was fast and athletic, but I was still trying to master the game and get my footwork into basketball mode.

I had grown irritated with Coach Smiley repeatedly telling me I was traveling with the ball. The first time he told me I was traveling, I got so excited. I thought he was taking me somewhere in his car. I discovered pretty quickly that he was talking about me moving my feet while holding the ball without dribbling it.

Still, why did he have to bring up traveling?

When I wasn't training with Coach Smiley, one of the guys from my village – a 20-something local basketball player named Barry – offered to work with me to strengthen my weaknesses. Sometimes, I walked with him to the University of West Indies campus, and he helped me improve my dribbling and shooting. Barry was passionate about the game of basketball, and he didn't want me to miss out on this opportunity.

Coach Hudson's promise gave me hope, and Coach Smiley and Barry believed in me, so I was determined to make basketball my path to success.

Basketball became my main focus. My everything.

On my long walks home from training with Coach Smiley, when I was drained from fatigue, I would ask God for strength to allow me to continue. I felt that God finally heard my prayers, as evidenced by this opportunity to escape poverty. I was patiently waiting to learn a sport I didn't even know anything about only a short time ago. I knew this was bigger than me and, for that reason, I couldn't take it for granted.

Although it was repetitive, each day of training became harder and even more intense than the day before. Nevertheless, I was training myself out of the ghetto, not because I didn't love where I was from, but because I wanted more than it could ever offer. I felt that Gola had prepared me for the outside world and I could survive anywhere.

Since I was showing improvement, Coach Smiley recommended me to join a basketball club in August Town called the Mustangs Phillies in order to help me learn organized basketball within a team and league environment. This gave me the drive to shake off any belief that I was unworthy of this chance. This team of young adult women was open and inviting to me and instantly made me feel like I belonged. They were patient with my newness to the game and impressed with my height. Most of my new teammates had been playing basketball for a long time and knew the game well. Mommy proudly bought me my first pair of basketball shoes.

The shoes were lightweight and relatively hard on my feet, but they were far better than playing barefoot. I came on the team pretty raw, and it was still challenging to dribble and maintain the ball. I was used to training with Coach Smiley without a backboard, and now I was practicing with the Mustangs Phillies with a backboard. Because of my training without a backboard, my shots were more accurate which gave me an advantage over other players. At six-foot-four, I could easily grab the rim, so I got to the rebound first most times.

With the basketball club, I was able to practice inside on a concrete floor, even though it was pretty hot and humid in the gym, which had no air-conditioning. The building also had some issues with its roof. When it rained, we placed buckets on the floor to catch the water leaking from the roof, then we wiped the floor and kept practicing.

Regardless of the challenging game and leaking roof, I enjoyed every minute of learning and playing this game.

At our first Mustangs Phillies game, lo and behold, I realized my opponents included those two intimidating female bullies who had shown up on my very first day of training with Coach Smiley. How could it be anything but a nightmare having to play against them in this, my first game? As to be expected, they were extra rough and tried to embarrass me by laughing at me throughout the game, calling me clumsy and weak. One in particular, who was twice my size in weight, was playing really physically rough against me, finally knocking me down by bumping me with her extra-large breasts. The referee shouted, "Foul with the breasts," and the crowd burst out laughing. I had to restrain my own laughter. I wasn't prepared to fight back against breasts. What was I supposed to do if she did that breast bump again?

Although I was missing some shots in the game, I was making several rebounds. I couldn't help but think that the one thing I was teased about my whole life – my height – was beginning to be the very thing that could help carry me through my life.

My teammates were clueless about the way our opponents had bullied me on my first day of training, since I never shared the situation with them, but it was clear that those bullies had mean-girl reputations. My team encouraged me to blow them off and focus on the game.

We ended up losing the game, but I finished with the most rebounds for both teams. I had found my strength in rebounding and definitely wasn't trying to get knocked out by breasts while on the court.

While I had that spark of excitement from playing my first-ever basketball game, on the bus ride home I was sad that we lost and that I was unable to contribute more to get a victory. Those bullies had gotten under my skin and touched the raw nerve of my self-doubt. I sat on the bus, strongly contemplating giving up.

Consumed once again by uncertainty, I wondered if perhaps those two intimidating bullies were right; maybe I was too clumsy and weak to play the game. But, once again, the voice within me reminded me that if I gave up, those bullies would win. I hated losing. I mean, I really hated losing as an athlete. I loved that sense of accomplishment winning gave me. It was so much better than the feeling of blowing out the back of my shoes and hiding or walking hunched down. Then it really hit me. In my first game ever, I had the most rebounds of anyone who played that day.

I held onto that positive perception of my performance in the game. I couldn't hold back a smile of humbled self-recognition. I saw myself for a moment in the same way many others were seeing me, and it felt good.

When I got off the bus from the game, I just wanted to see Mama Nancy. She always knew how to make me feel better. Mama Nancy supported my angry and hurt side, advising me not to let anyone push me around, while mommy appealed to my more thoughtful side, advising me to ignore them and stay focused. At this point, I just wanted the doubters and bullies to leave me alone, soon as possible. No delays. I was 17 years old and desperate to escape Gola and help my family. I couldn't tolerate people trying to stand in my way. Those girls really, deeply got under my skin.

I soon became the number one shot-blocker and rebounder with the Mustangs Phillies basketball club, and at 17, I was recruited in May 1991 to join the Jamaican Women's National Basketball

Team. This team represented Jamaica in international competitions, principally in the Caribbean. Being chosen was a huge feat for me because I was recruited to join the Jamaican national team in the same year I had learned the game of basketball. My mind was in a fog with all these new experiences, all this recognition and success. I knew this was very unusual to accomplish in such a short time, and I had a hard time processing it all. As a high school senior on the Jamaican Women's National Basketball Team, I was the youngest player. I was so proud to represent my country, my family, and Gola on this team. Everything just kept getting more and more unreal.

As my skills greatly improved, I contacted Coach Hudson again around May 1991 to follow up on my scholarship offer. With this call, I was so excited to take the next step in fulfilling this amazing dream, but I learned instead that he had decided to not offer me the scholarship. I was devastated by his words. Stunned. All that work, fueled by the intensity of my dreams, and the opportunity was just squashed in a single phone call. Speechless, I cried quietly on my end of the line.

But he had more to say.

He told me that he wanted me to attend a junior college in Oklahoma for my first two years, so I could refine my skills before attending the University of Oklahoma. He had asked Brad Walck, the women's head coach at Seminole Junior College in Seminole, Oklahoma, to consider signing me to a full scholarship.

I breathed a sigh of relief.

In June 1991, Coach Walck contacted Coach Smiley and decided to visit Kingston to watch me play in the Jamaican Women's National Basketball Team's three-day tournament that was coming up in a few weeks, in hopes of recruiting me to play for his college team. However, my renewed excitement and hope soon changed to anxiety and depression because, much to my surprise, I was benched in the first game and never got any playing time.

As I sat on the bench in disbelief and total embarrassment, I watched the more seasoned players on the court. I asked the coach when I would be put into the game? I repeated to the coach that a college coach from America was sitting in the stands to watch me play for a scholarship opportunity. Still, I was not put into the game. The longer I sat, the more upset I became that I was not being allowed to play. Coach Walck sat in the bleachers and watched me sit on the bench game after game.

It was the final day of the tournament. I was scared and pretty certain that I was going to lose my scholarship opportunity if Coach Walck never got a chance to see if I even knew how to play. I felt betrayed because the Jamaican Women's National Basketball Team's coach knew why Coach Walck was there, but still wasn't allowing me to showcase my skills.

As I watched the timer tick down, I realized that I wasn't going to play, not even for a minute. I couldn't see why Coach Walck would want to recruit me after seeing me do nothing, seemingly thought so little of by my coach that I never even touched the court during competition. All the work and sacrifice that I put into learning the game from Coach Smiley had prepared me for the opportunity I thought the tournament provided. Yet, for some unknown and unfathomable reason, I was unable to show any of what I'd learned to Coach Walck, who came to the tournament specifically to see me play.

When Coach Walck, who was six-foot-three with dirty blonde hair, walked up to me after the game, I apologized for wasting his time.

He said, "Apologize for what? I watched you closely during warmups, and I want to offer you a scholarship."

I couldn't believe he was still interested. My dream of playing in America was alive again. I had a huge smile, which seemed stuck to my face, and thanked him repeatedly. The hurt and anger of not playing was replaced with joy and appreciation. I couldn't wait to tell everyone I knew. Coach Walck, for some unexplainable reason, had just offered me a chance at a whole new life, an opportunity to be more than my school principal, perhaps, ever expected me to be.

For the second time after a devastating sports failure, someone told me that they thought I was great and wanted to offer me a scholarship. How ironic is that? They saw something in me that I didn't see in myself.

I often heard people speak of how America is filled with opportunities. I was ready to find each and every one of those opportunities. In that moment of defeat leading to opportunity, I promised myself that someday I would represent my country again on the Jamaican Women's National Basketball Team – and not as a bench player.

The Monday following the tournament, I was back in school and feeling extremely proud and excited about my future for the first time. Even though I was a part of the KT track team, I had learned the game of basketball, and it clearly was my future. Consequently, I focused on getting ever better at basketball. I was excited to continue practicing the sport.

I told the coach of our school's boys basketball team that I was offered a scholarship and asked him if I could train with the team on their outside courts. He agreed. It was close to the end of my senior year, and there were no girls basketball teams in high schools across the island. My only opportunity to be challenged by people my age was to practice with the boys.

I was nervous joining the boys practice for the first time. When I walked up, still wearing my school uniform, some players shouted that they didn't want a girl to practice with them, although I was taller than everyone else there. I ignored them and spoke to some players that I knew from track and field. Growing up with three brothers, I was used to feeling excluded because I was a girl. When the boys were short on players, I played with them, and to protect their fragile male egos, I passed the ball to them, even when I figured I could make the basket.

It was unbearably hot outside while I played with the boys' team and felt as if the sun was melting my skin. Some of them were purposely rough with me since my height enabled me to block their shots, but it was teaching me how to be a physically stronger player and more competitive.

Schoolgirls stood on the side watching the boys, and I could hear them whispering about me, as though they were shocked that I was playing with the boys. I was mentally strong enough to handle them.

The boys hit me harder and harder, and I was learning how to take their hits. No one on the basketball team knew that I was offered the scholarship. Only the coach knew. I didn't want to risk hearing negative comments, so I kept it to myself. By the end of practice, I finally earned the respect of a team that I didn't even play for, despite being a girl, because they liked that I didn't back down. They slowly but surely started to welcome me onto their boys' basketball team, unofficially.

Coach Walck was still in town, making repeated attempts to retrieve my high school transcripts from my principal, but to no avail. For some reason, my principal, who should have been deeply proud for me and helping me in any way an educator can help a student to work for and achieve their dreams, was instead being uncooperative in assisting the coach in acquiring all my necessary academic records.

I complained to my parents, and daddy and mommy went to the school office to request my academic records. However, they had no more influence or luck than Coach Walck, who had to extend his stay in Kingston for two extra days.

He finally succeeded in obtaining my academic records. The documents were required by the NCAA rules committee for me to receive the scholarship. When he finally had my academic records, he then officially offered me the full scholarship to play as a forward-center. I couldn't wait to tell mommy the good news.

"Mommy, I got the basketball scholarship in America!"

She said, "Lord, have mercy. That's good Simi." She was happy, yet noticeably disappointed because receiving the scholarship meant I had to leave her. It was bittersweet since I had to leave before my high school graduation and she wanted to see me graduate, as did daddy and Mama Nancy.

Coach Walck came to our house for mommy to sign my letter of intent. "Since you cared enough to come all the way to Kingston, then I will trust you to watch over her in America."

But, I am pretty sure he didn't mind coming to beautiful Jamaica.

CHAPTER 6

CHASING THE AMERICAN DREAM

In August 1991, my dream to live in America was about to come true. Mommy had prepared me as best as she could to take on the world. I said my goodbyes to family and friends, and as I was about to leave Kingston, mommy gave me priceless advice. She said, "Don't go there and lose your way. Stay focused, and don't forget why you're there." And off I flew to America.

When I first arrived in Seminole, Oklahoma, I had on my best clothes – a pant suit mommy had sewn for me – because we were taught growing up that Americans dressed well. Mommy wanted me to fit in as best as I could. However, when I landed, everyone was dressed like the cowboys in all those American movies I had watched growing up, wearing jeans, work shirts, and cowboy hats. Seminole was less than one percent "other races," and I was considered one of the "other races." I was six-foot-four Jamaican, and, although noticeable, I didn't fit in anywhere.

I wondered where the skyscrapers and expensive cars were that I had seen on television. I was in the middle of nowhere, seemingly, and oddly, I was surrounded by familiar accents from growing up and watching cowboy and Indian television shows.

I started out learning about my new home by doing what was familiar to me – walking. I began walking around the campus and up and down the road near the campus. I looked for a bus stop, but there were none to be found.

Seminole was so different from Kingston. There was no one on the side of the road selling food and no barefoot women sitting outside their homes chatting away. There were no gunmen walking around, no loud music playing out in the road, and no fruit trees. It was so quiet in Seminole. I could hear my own heart beating.

I was in culture shock, realizing that not only was I foreign, but there weren't any people who even looked like me. I quickly came to sense the challenges were tenfold more than what I'd expected. I felt alone.

I came to America with what seemed like a fortune to me, $100, and I knew mommy couldn't afford to send me money often. Mommy's income was not enough to transfer over into U.S. dollars, and daddy was similarly struggling to make ends meet.

I didn't have any clothes for the upcoming winter. I only packed the summer clothes I had, which were year-round attire in Kingston.

I was lonesome, nervous and anxious, yet excited. There was no turning back now. I was now, officially, a Seminole Junior College student-athlete, and I had to learn what all that meant, what all that entailed.

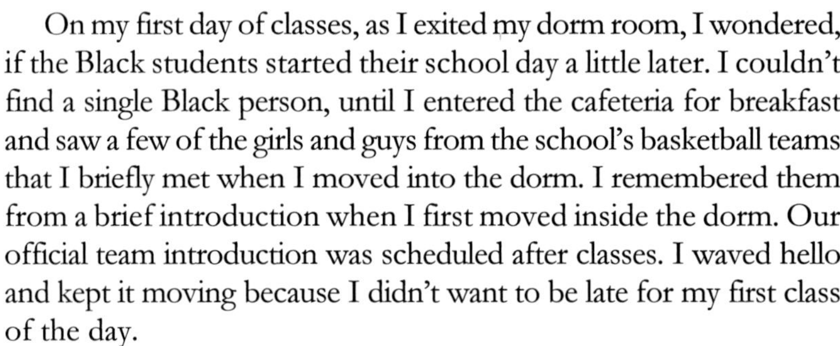

On my first day of classes, as I exited my dorm room, I wondered, if the Black students started their school day a little later. I couldn't find a single Black person, until I entered the cafeteria for breakfast and saw a few of the girls and guys from the school's basketball teams that I briefly met when I moved into the dorm. I remembered them from a brief introduction when I first moved inside the dorm. Our official team introduction was scheduled after classes. I waved hello and kept it moving because I didn't want to be late for my first class of the day.

As I headed to my first class, I got lost, even though it was a small campus. I stopped by the campus bookstore to ask for directions and saw this Native American girl, who I had seen earlier at my dorm. She stayed two doors down from my room, but we hadn't introduced ourselves to each other. I walked over to her and realized she was working in the store as a cashier. She was so fascinating to me because she looked just like the Native Americans I used to watch on television back home.

I introduced myself to her, and she said her name was Jamie. *Jamie?* I expected her to have a unique Native American name from the cowboys and Indians television shows I was accustomed to. I asked her for directions to my first class, and she kindly obliged. Thanking her, I hurried along, arriving at my first class on time.

It was American History. They didn't talk much about Blacks or Native Americans, which was interesting in its glaring absence. I figured I had enough time to learn about everyone in America while I was here, but first I would have to understand their strong, country accents.

The first basketball team meeting was held right after my last class. I walked to the gym, the Raymond Harber Fieldhouse had a seating capacity for 1,000 people. The exterior of the building had tan bricks, and the gym was attached to the swimming pool natatorium. As I entered the building, there was a large lobby with concession stands and a huge trophy case with pictures of former teams, signed basketballs, and trophies. There were four locker rooms, four coaches' offices, a weight room, training room, and two classrooms.

As I entered the gym, I gazed at the beautiful, smooth and shiny maple hardwood floor. The gym was not as big and overwhelming as the University of Oklahoma's basketball gym, but it was way better than the outdoor, concrete courts in Kingston. It made me appreciate my humble beginnings. A few of the girls were shooting around. Some were talking on the court, while others were sitting in the bleachers. Coach Walck began the meeting by advising us that this was his first year as the Seminole Belles women's head coach. Although the previous head coach had signed several players before he left, Coach Walck had seven of 15 scholarships left to fill. He told us that Seminole Junior College was one of the first colleges to give full athletic scholarships to women.

Coach Walck then let us introduce ourselves individually to our teammates. Most of the players were freshmen, and three were sophomores. He then handed out our pre-season workout training schedule for the next two months, which showed mostly conditioning work.

After the team meeting, I walked around the campus to take it all in. It was still all so unreal. I couldn't believe I was here in this small, rural town for basketball – a game I never knew until a year ago.

As I tried adjusting to a new culture with all the unfamiliar foods and lifestyles, I had trouble adapting and accepting the overwhelming amount of new and unfamiliar. With no one to understand the isolation I was experiencing adapting to my new surroundings, I quickly grew stressed. I didn't know how to address my culture shock to let out some of that anxious, gnawing energy I felt. Coach Walck noticed something was wrong, and introduced me to our school counselor, Tracy. She was about five-feet tall with blonde hair, and I towered over her as we introduced ourselves. She was welcoming and as sweet as can be.

Moving to a new country, I kept to myself most of the time. I felt homesick, missing my culture, family, friends, and food. I missed all that I knew. Everything was so unfamiliar, and I knew no one. Day after day, I felt more comfortable to speak freely around my school counselor. She encouraged me to make the most of my college experience, and I tried my best to follow suit.

Our first official basketball practice was on October 1, 1991. Coach Walck handed out the team practice gear before practice. I was elated, since each player received shorts, a jersey, socks, shirts, warm-ups, jackets, fleece pants and a pair of Nike shoes. My first pair of name-brand, quality, comfortable, and supportive shoes. As other players may have worn their warm-ups as a display of school spirit and team pride, I could use mine to now fit in and not have to wear my worn clothing around campus.

I anticipated playing basketball for our first practice, but Coach Walck had other plans. We performed more conditioning. Some of the girls didn't like all the conditioning, but I didn't mind because

I came to Seminole already in great shape. It was to my advantage that I had walked daily since I was 4 years old.

Coach Walck also went over fundamentals. He wanted our skills to be fundamentally sound before the season started in a month. I wasn't too proud to ask Coach Walck to work with me on fundamentals, so he spent extra time with me to work on my post moves. I needed to work on the drop step – a move stretching my leg to one side while dribbling the ball and turning towards the basket and the turnaround jump shot. It involved turning in the air, and timing the jump shot when the defender is not likely to jump and challenge the shot.

Although I had a long way to go, basketball became my escape and main focus. Knowing no one and finding nothing familiar, the basketball court became my familiar place, where I could let off steam while focusing on getting even better at this still relatively new game to me. While focused on basketball, my mind was distracted from the gnawing sense of homesickness I felt.

Within two months of my arrival, it was finally time for our first game. I woke up on the morning of that first game, feeling gazillions of butterflies inside my stomach. This was it. All the work I had put in with Coach Smiley, Barry and the Mustangs Phillies, Coach Walck and alone shooting inside the Harber Fieldhouse gym was going to be put on display in a few hours.

Before the game and after our shoot-around, Coach Walck walked us through our game plan. I imagined my family and friends sitting inside the gym, enthusiastically cheering me on. I so wished they could have been there. Having just one of them present would have been perfect.

Now it was game time, and I watched fans pouring in, curious to see what the new coach and team had to offer. I watched the girls from the opposing team warming up on the other end of the court. There was no one there as tall as I was. I knew immediately that I had a height advantage.

As I was heading out on to the court, I took deep breaths, reassuring myself that I could do this. On the court, I could hear

Coach Walck shouting for me to block the shots. As hard as it was to not get distracted by the cheering crowd, I knew I had to focus on the game. I started running the floor for lay ups and repeatedly grabbed rebounds. I braved my first college game, and we won.

We went on to win the first five games of the season before losing to Connors State College from Warner, Oklahoma, in a close game. The games became harder and harder, and I also became better as the season progressed.

The games built my self-confidence on the court. But after the games and cheers were over, I returned to my dorm room alone. It was in the dorm that I was most conscious of being socially isolated. To relieve the boredom, I'd go for long walks, just to get out of the small space and be surrounded by people, yet I still felt so alone.

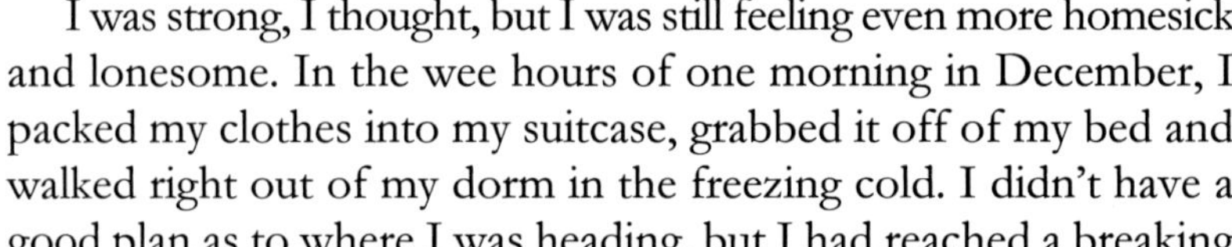

I was strong, I thought, but I was still feeling even more homesick and lonesome. In the wee hours of one morning in December, I packed my clothes into my suitcase, grabbed it off of my bed and walked right out of my dorm in the freezing cold. I didn't have a good plan as to where I was heading, but I had reached a breaking point. I began walking close to the state highway that ran near the dorm, broken and determined that I needed to go back home.

A few of my teammates noticed me on the highway and tried to get me to go back to my dorm room, but I refused. About a half hour later, Coach Walck's car pulled up along the highway and he demanded that I get inside. He proceeded to drive me to his office. Truth is, he was already growing frustrated with me because it wasn't the first time that I had threatened to go home. I was becoming a pain to him with my constant state of stress and upset. His face was beet red, and his eyes were squinting from his interruption of sleep. He shouted, "Simone, I am calling the airline to make reservations for a plane ticket to Jamaica."

I broke down and cried uncontrollably. "I can't go home," I said. "My mommy will kill me!" I wasn't just alone here but trapped, feeling like I couldn't possibly go home and disappoint mommy. I didn't know how to endure this confusion and isolation. Although

Coach Walck had an open-door policy to his office, and Tracey was welcoming, I wasn't use to sharing my internal struggles. I eventually opened up to him sharing that I was just not adapting well. I told him that if I had no money and was hungry after the cafeteria closed, I had no way to eat. I was extremely hungry after practices and drills, and the unfamiliar American food didn't stay down. I finally shared with him the seemingly overwhelming challenges of my new cultural experiences in Seminole.

After our emotional talk, in which I finally shared this gnawing, hammering burden, he understood much better what I was experiencing. That breakdown was a cry for help that resulted in a release of a lot of unresolved anxiety and confusion. His voice suddenly turned from stern to sympathetic. I never went walking at night again – and certainly not on the dangerous highway. I missed picking fruits or buying a sky juice for 10 cents or a slice of buttered bread for 25 cents. This wasn't the America I'd dreamt about.

The NCAA scholarship was a wonderful gift, but had its disadvantages. Their rules were that no one associated with the school could assist a scholarship student athlete to meet the challenge of hunger, whether they were living far away from home, far away from family or just flat-out poor. There were no resources to help. The scholarship helped me live in America, but it was keeping me from building any kind of support network of people who could voluntarily help a poor, foreign student thrive in America.

Because of this, even when Coach Walck told me he wanted me to meet Bonnie Ritchie, the lady who supervised the cafeteria, I was rather skeptical of her ability to help me. There wasn't much she could do in reference to my needs, according to the NCAA. I was told by Coach Walck that Bonnie Ritchie and her husband were huge Seminole basketball fans.

I went to introduce myself to Bonnie at the cafeteria, and she gave me the warmest greeting. She was a middle-aged, six-foot-one, slender lady with short dirty blonde hair, who sweetly asked how she could help me. I told her that I just wanted to eat chicken and rice, since chicken in most any form was my favorite food.

Soon after, as Bonnie and I bonded, I met her equally welcoming husband Herman. Bonnie became a mother figure to me in this small community. With this new sense of family, I took my course work even more seriously. I worked just as hard in my classes as I did in the gym. Not only did my professors start complimenting my work ethic, but I ultimately became one of the most recognizable athletes on campus.

The team was slowly jelling much better, and we were winning a majority of our games. In practice, I often outran my teammates down the floor, grabbing the rim and showing how high I could jump. As we approached midseason, Coach Walck designed his offense and defense around me. I was improving my game as I put in a lot of extra work. I spoke to my teammates more off the court and had gotten to know them better with all the traveling, training, and games we had together. Most of the girls were kind, but definitely not all. Some of my teammates just didn't accept me for some reason or another. Since I came from Jamaica, a few of my teammates taunted me with questions, asking whether I grew up swinging on trees or did we have cars, as if Jamaicans were animals or primitive. I defended my country and educated them about what we had, since I felt they were just as misinformed about Jamaica as I was about Indians. But, it didn't take long to realize they were just trying to be cruel at my expense. This hostile treatment was all too familiar to me, and I had to wonder if the lack of acceptance toward me was largely because of my popularity and media attention as a newbie player.

As usual, bullies' taunts motivated me. I kept focused on being even more successful than my first year. They didn't see me training in the gym during my downtime while they were enjoying their social lives. Up to that point in my life, all I'd ever wanted to be was accepted and not bullied, and I had convinced myself for some time that if I got stronger and better, then my teammates would respect me. But it really didn't matter at what level I played, or how good I got, there were still people who taunted me. I no longer desired their acceptance. Bullying was a reflection of the bully, not of me. To finally understand that was liberating.

Since Seminole Junior College was a two-year college, I only had two seasons there, then I planned to transfer to the University of Oklahoma to play for Coach Hudson. So, I had to push myself even harder. We completed our first season with a 27-5 record. We had a perfect 10-0 Conference record and finished the season ranked in the National Junior College Athletic Association (NJCAA) Top 10.

Coach Walck called me to his office. "Simone, you were named NJCAA Second Team All-American," he said. I swiftly responded, "No, Coach. I'm All-Jamaican." I didn't understand for the life of me why I would be named an American. Coach Walck laughed longer than he should have. I stood there in a state of confusion. He finally stopped laughing, looked at me and start laughing all over again. I didn't know whether to laugh with him or run out of his office. After he finally came up for air, he explained that All-Americans were voted as the best players in the country. Then, I joined him in laughter.

He presented me with a plaque and its accompanying announcement letter, and I proudly brought it to my dorm room. I couldn't wait to write to my family back home to share the exciting news. I wanted so badly to use the payphone outside my dorm room, where I sometimes received calls from mommy and daddy, but I didn't have any more money. I was always excited whenever I got a call. I was excited right then, but I couldn't make a phone call.

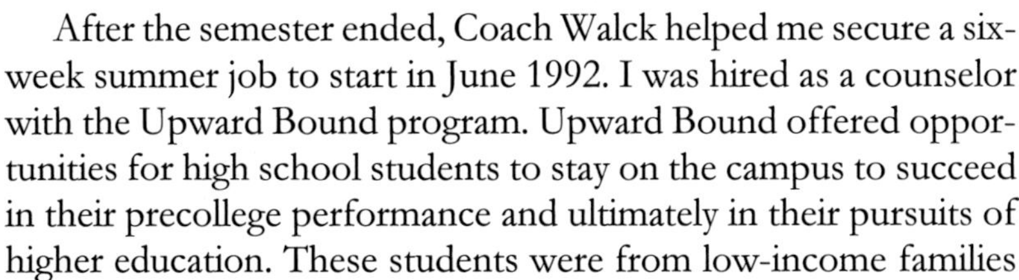

After the semester ended, Coach Walck helped me secure a six-week summer job to start in June 1992. I was hired as a counselor with the Upward Bound program. Upward Bound offered opportunities for high school students to stay on the campus to succeed in their precollege performance and ultimately in their pursuits of higher education. These students were from low-income families and/or families in which neither parent held a college degree. My own path had similarities to the profiles of these students, as my family was low-income and neither of my parents held a college degree. I came to really enjoy paying it forward and working with the high school students in the program.

Consequently, I found out about a summer basketball league called the American Athletic Union, otherwise known as the AAU. The AAU was an amateur sports organization dedicated exclusively to the promotion and development of amateur sports, which was perfect for continual training. While playing on a team in the AAU, I befriended one of my teammates, a high-schooler named Devon Balfour. She had blonde hair and blue eyes and was the opposite of a cowgirl. We became like sisters in a short span. Between Upward Bound and AAU, giving back, basketball development, and unexpected friendships, things were looking up for me in Seminole.

After saving my paychecks from Upward Bound, I wanted to use some of my earnings to go shopping for some much-needed items as well as articles to take back with me to Jamaica. Ever since I arrived on campus, I'd overhear students mentioning a store called Walmart. It was the biggest store in Seminole, so clearly, I wanted to go.

I asked one of my teammates, Nicole Anderson, who everyone called Nicki, to drive me to Walmart. Nicki was a true cowgirl, who stood at about five-foot-eleven. She was a dirty blonde who always cracked jokes. Nicki and I went on joyrides often, including to her family home in Prague, about 20 minutes from Seminole. Her mother Peggy prepared home-cooked meals, her father Dave was a big guy with a great sense of humor, and her older brother Doug opened their home to me, and I never once felt unwanted.

On our drive to Walmart, as usual, she only played country songs. I would sing along to popular country artists, such as Garth Brooks and my favorite artist, Reba McEntire. Once inside Walmart, I ran from aisle to aisle like a big kid. I was so in awe of the selection of merchandise that I didn't know exactly how to process it, nor did I want to leave.

About an hour later, I heard my name over the loud Walmart intercom. "Will Simone Edwards please report to the front of the store? Will Simone Edwards please report to the front of the store?"

I was sitting on bicycles because I'd never owned one. A few minutes later, I heard my name called over the intercom, again.

As it turns out, Nicki had been looking all over the store for me. How hard is it to miss a six-foot-four Jamaican girl sitting on bicycles in Walmart in rural Seminole? After I made my way to the cash register, I was eager to try out the flavored, colored toothpaste I'd just purchased because, in Jamaica, I only ever used white, tasteless toothpaste. I bought 10 tubes, so I could give them as gifts to my family and friends back home. The cashier added everything up, and then surprising added even more to it. I expected the total cost to be exactly what was on the products. I already knew how much money I had in my pocket, and it wasn't the amount she told me. I argued with the cashier that she was making a mistake because I had already added everything up in my head, and her numbers were wrong.

Seeing my confusion about the final price, Nicki politely intervened and kindly paid the extra amount. I learned about sales taxes that day. And, I wasn't too pleased.

It was fall 1992, and my final season and school year at Seminole Junior College.

I intended to be even better my final season.

I bonded with a Japanese international student, Elliko Fujiwara, who lived two doors down from my dorm room, initially because she became our new basketball team manager. Since we were both international students adapting to American culture, we could relate to each other and, through that shared awkwardness, formed a strong friendship. We spoke often about our cultures and upbringings as she shared Japanese candies that her family mailed to her. During our free time, Elliko rebounded the ball for me while I worked on my shots and free throws. She chastised me for missing free throws, pushing me to stay focused.

Jamie, the Native American campus bookstore cashier, lived in the adjoining room to Elliko. As a consequence of shared living space, we all bonded and became close friends. Jamie began taking me to Powwows. Both of them helped me come out of my protective shell and reach into the world to make new friends who may not have looked like me but shared important things with me that bonded us and helped us all feel at ease about our experience in Seminole.

One afternoon, there was a knock on my dorm room door. I couldn't believe my eyes. Coach Smiley was standing next to Coach Walck with a big smile. I screamed with excitement and embraced him. Unbeknownst to me, Coach Walck offered Coach Smiley a job as student assistant for both the men's and women's basketball programs, and he had accepted and relocated to Seminole. Coach Walck was highly impressed that Coach Smiley trained me in such a short time and felt he could benefit from Coach Smiley's developmental skills at Seminole Junior College.

Coach Smiley was not only a coach, he was like a big brother to me. I was elated to have someone from back home in Seminole. I was certain to be an even better player with him around. His presence gave me the extra drive and momentum I needed to push for even greater excellence, and he was eager to help me develop further as a player.

The basketball season was approaching, and my statistics were impressive, which led to even more media in the local and school newspapers. As my basketball success rose, so did bad attitudes from a few of my teammates. Some of them claimed that I was being treated better than they were because I was the star of the team, while others alleged that my grades were good since the professors were big basketball fans. As much I wished that was the case, I was the first one in the gym every day and stayed to shoot after everyone left. I lifted weights on my days off and spent countless hours in the library with tutors. But I didn't care to explain these truths to any of them. At this point, the bitter teammates became less relevant since I now had a good support system with my new friends, welcoming homes, and Coach Smiley.

It was November 1992, a day before our first game of the season and time for practice. My menstruation started unexpectedly. I was out of sanitary napkins and all my friends were in practice, so I ran to the nearest store, which was one mile away.

I finally arrived at practice, 30 minutes late panicking because I figured I'd be in trouble. I was out of breath and cramping. This was my first tardiness at Seminole Junior College and uncharacteristic of me. My teammates were on the court, and I could see the disappointment in the eyes of both Coach Walck and Coach Smiley, but all I honestly wanted to do was rip out my female organs. Coach Walck chose to abide by his strict rules on tardiness by not starting me in our first game of the season.

Many of the fans who attended the women's games were expecting me to start. It was tough on me to sit and watch the game from the bench. I sat on the bench the entire first half. I understood punishing players for tardiness, but I was thinking to myself that this punishment was rather harsh for a first-time offense.

In the second half, I got in the game. I ended up having a good game because I knew how important it was to also make my statement on the court. I thought, or maybe I hoped, that Coach Walck would've just made me run as punishment, but he knew that would have been far too easy for me.

I didn't tell either coach why I was late. I just accepted the punishment, as I had done the one time I was late for my first practice with Coach Smiley. Not starting bothered me mainly because I relished the indescribable feeling of hearing my name called in the starting five.

Apart from basketball, I started participating in on-campus events, such as line-dancing inside the cafeteria on certain days. They cleared the tables and brought out the cowboys and cowgirls. I was right in the middle, overlooking the crowd due to my height, performing a line dance that Nicki taught me. Everyone cheered me on, and I had a good ol' time. I was more visible because of the team's success and my popularity as a player.

One particular day while walking on campus, I saw flyers posted promoting a college talent show. It was just days before the Christmas break. I told my friends we should attend, but Nicki suggested that I enter the talent competition solely based on our sing-a-longs in her car. Even though I knew I wasn't much of a singer, I considered it. I am certain she thought I was a good entertainer, so I entered the talent show.

I was first introduced to country music as a child, as mommy had a real liking for it. For the talent show, I decided to perform an Oklahoma favorite, *You Never Gave Up On Me,* by Crystal Gayle, which reminded me of mommy since this was a song she played on her old record player.

The performance took place in the school auditorium. Around 100 attendees were there. I got on stage, feeling confident relishing the attention. I went up to the microphone and did a whole teary-eyed speech dedicating the songs to my friends who had become my rich support system in Seminole. I began singing and, as I looked out in the audience, Nicki and Elliko were crying. When I was finished, I got a standing ovation from my friends, as they were cheering wildly.

All of the contestants lined up to hear our fate. "Simone Edwards, first place," the host announced. First place in a talent show? Maybe I wasn't as bad a singer as I thought I was. Still, no more talent shows for me. I knew to stop while I was on top. I proudly took my trophy and placed it next to my Second Team All-American plaque in my dorm room.

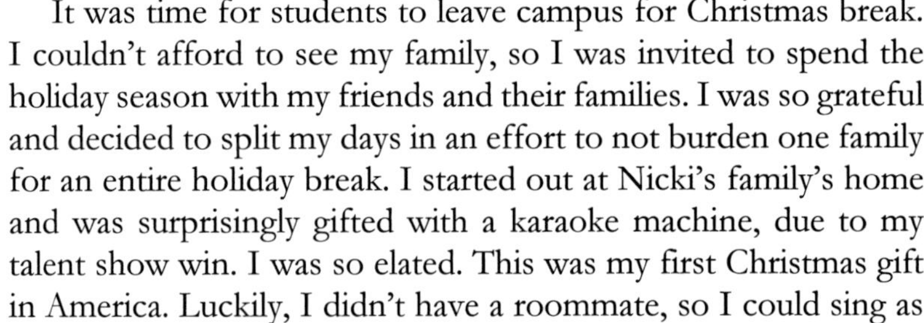

It was time for students to leave campus for Christmas break. I couldn't afford to see my family, so I was invited to spend the holiday season with my friends and their families. I was so grateful and decided to split my days in an effort to not burden one family for an entire holiday break. I started out at Nicki's family's home and was surprisingly gifted with a karaoke machine, due to my talent show win. I was so elated. This was my first Christmas gift in America. Luckily, I didn't have a roommate, so I could sing as loud as I wanted with my new gift.

After a day with Nicki and her family, Devon, from my AAU team, offered to pick me up. Devon and I hadn't seen each other since summer, although we kept in touch by phone. When Devon pulled up, we started screaming in excitement and hugged each other. Our drive to her house took about an hour. It was out in the country, sitting on about an acre of land. When we arrived, we got out of the car, and I saw two giant dogs running toward us. I nearly crapped my pants and made a U-turn back inside the car, refusing to come out. I had never seen dogs that big in my life. Devon said they were friendly and would only lick me to death. But, I wasn't taking any chances since I was almost scared to death.

Her family came out of the house to greet me, although I hoped they were there to rescue me. I was greeted by the Balfour family – her stepmother Joann, her father Bill, and her sisters, Rachelle, Aryn, and Jill. They were all very warm and welcoming, but I refused to get out of the car with the dogs that were as tall as I was. Sure, they were beautiful dogs, but their teeth were beautifully scary. Devon's family laughed, but I wasn't getting out of the car. They finally caved in and put the dogs away.

After the dogs were ushered away, I came out of the car, and the family all hugged me as if they had known me for years. I immediately let down my guard and walked with them into the house, more than ready to eat, since I smelled chicken cooking in the oven before I even entered their home.

Once inside, Joann, who had a strong country accent and the warmest of hearts, told me that their home was my home, too, so if I needed anything to eat, to help myself. She was obviously quite unfamiliar with how I ate when she offered that gracious gift of hospitality. Then, I was taken to Devon's room, where I placed my bag. Her room had a bunk bed. We were going to be roommates for the weekend and hoped to catch up some more on her season at her high school and mine at Seminole.

When dinner was ready, we all found seats in the living room. The chicken was delicious, along with the entire meal that Joann cooked for the family that day. As I was on my fifth piece of chicken, the family started asking me questions about Jamaica and my time in Seminole. I thought to myself, this tactic may have been to limit my chicken intake, because I was doing most of the talking. Pleasant, warm, and maybe a little crafty?

After dinner, Devon and I stayed up nearly all night talking. She was on the top bunk, and I was on the bottom with my feet hanging over. We finally fell asleep only to shortly be awakened by Joann telling us that breakfast was ready.

It was Christmas morning. There was a big Christmas tree in the living room with many presents piled under the tree, and I was in awe when I noticed that my name was on many of them. Devon must have told them I didn't have much. I was so overwhelmed. It felt so warm and wonderful, but it also made me feel homesick. I missed my family in the midst of such holiday splendor, and it had nothing to do with gifts.

In the Balfour home, there was a sense of family. I excused myself and hurried to the bathroom to cry. I quickly dried my eyes and returned to their festive family gathering as if nothing had happened. I really appreciated the love they were showing me and was overcome with emotion. I was gifted a blue soft robe, winter socks, thermal underwear, and various articles that were helpful for the brutal Oklahoma winter. I had never received this many presents in one setting.

It was my last semester at Seminole Junior College, and overall I had created a sense of belonging on and off campus. Since I never had the chance to learn to drive, I was eager to learn. I befriended an African American track student-athlete named Barbara "Barb" Cudjo, who agreed to teach me. Most of my friends in Seminole learned how drive while they were in high school. But mommy had never had a car. So, this opportunity to learn to drive was exciting, but also a bit terrifying.

Barb was patient with me, teaching me to drive in empty parking lots where I often jerked her car around, pressing the brakes too hard and too quickly. After days of driving lessons, Barb finally felt comfortable enough to take me out on the road.

So, we went out on the road and, as I put the car in reverse, I almost backed up into a ditch. She shouted, "STOP!" Nonetheless, Barb didn't give up teaching me until I finally, sort of, got the hang of it. And, after the second try, I was able to pass my driver's permit test.

Barb helped me significantly to understand the history of African Americans and their convoluted relationship to white Americans. I saw skin color because I have eyes, but I didn't see it in the same way Barb explained how some people in America saw skin color. I didn't grow up around racism, just classism and sexism since there was basically one race in Gola. I saw all my friends in Seminole as people with just different shades of complexion and cultures. I didn't care what color they were as long as they were good people. If someone wasn't nice, I just assumed they were just mean. I didn't yet comprehend the racism Barb had faced on a regular basis, until she explained it. I was only passing through this country, and Seminole was just my first stop.

Our team was now 10-0, and we were ranked #1 in the nation. Our gym was packed each game after becoming such a winning team. I averaged a double-double for the season, accumulating double-digit numbers in both rebounds and points per game. Therefore, I began to draw attention from numerous NCAA Division I universities. Recruiters sent letters, and Division I coaches called Coach Walck on a daily basis, but he told them I was verbally committed to the University of Oklahoma. Most of the top 20 schools contacted him about their chances of recruiting me. During my two years at Seminole Junior College, our team record was 56 wins and eight losses.

At the end of my final season, I was named the Regional Player of the Year, MVP, NJCAA All-American First Team and the first Kodak All-American in Seminole's school history. Coach Walck said I had turned the women's basketball program around. He and Coach Smiley believed in me, took time out to help me put in the extra work, and provided the support I needed to flourish.

My final year at Seminole Junior College turned out better than I could expected. As icing on the cake, mommy saved her money to attend graduation to see me accept my associate's degree. I hadn't seen her in two years. This was important for both of us, since she didn't get to see me walk at high school graduation. When she arrived, she stayed with me in my dorm room.

At the graduation, Bonnie and Herman invited mommy to sit next to them. I kept looking up at their seats, and I could see mommy's beaming smile. Being called on stage for my diploma was my gift to her. All I wanted to do was give her a big hug, but mommy was not one to hug or kiss. However, after the graduation, she grabbed me with the tightest embrace and planted a big kiss on my cheek. That very rare and most unexpected moment gave me a boost of inner strength that I needed to soar to higher heights. With tears in her eyes, mommy was extremely proud of her girl, and I was so overwhelmed to have experienced that moment with her. Seeing me in my cap and gown made her so overjoyed. I promised to continue to be even more of a reason for her smile and affection.

CHAPTER 7

HAWKEYE NATION

The plan after graduating from Seminole Junior College was to transfer to the University of Oklahoma to play for Coach Hudson. But, much to my dismay, Coach Walck informed me that Coach Hudson no longer worked at the University of Oklahoma. Since Coach Hudson was the only reason I was going to the University of Oklahoma, now I felt no obligation to attend.

Coach Walck was still receiving offer letters, so he helped me sort through them, reviewing them one by one. One of my early top picks was the University of Iowa (UI). Coach Marianna Freeman, an assistant basketball coach at UI recruited me after watching me play during the AAU competitions. Coach Freeman was a nice African American woman, who wore a mullet hairstyle. She told me about the head women's coach, C. Vivian Stringer, and the team. However, there was very little persuading needed since UI initially appealed to me because of Coach Stringer, who was the highest-profile coach of color in the nation in any sport, regardless of gender. I had seen her on television and knew that I wanted to play for her because she was a Black successful female coach.

The University of Iowa offered me a full scholarship, another absolute relief to me. On my first official visit, I met the legendary Coach Stringer during a one-on-one meeting. She made it clear to me in numerous ways that I was more than a six-foot-four, fast, Jamaican player to her. She was actually interested in hearing about my life, so I shared my life story from the beginning. She was so authentic and sincere, and I connected with her caring and genuine spirit instantly. I thought I could learn a lot about basketball from her. She reminded me of mommy in so many ways. She was strict, family-oriented and kind, and that was exactly what I needed at that time in my life.

Before officially accepting the offer from the University of Iowa, I decided to use up my five official visits to make sure I was making the best choice for me. One of my official visits was to Western Illinois University, since I was on the top of their recruiting list. I met with an African American women's head coach, Regina Miller, who represented herself and the university in a positive light, which impressed me. She gave me her undivided attention and was easy to talk to. I felt a good connection with her and was truly interested in her program. But, I was torn. When the visits were done, it was clearly time to decide.

I accepted the scholarship offer to join the Hawkeye nation at the University of Iowa. I just couldn't wait to play for Coach Stringer. However, it was very difficult to share my decision with Coach Miller, since she communicated with me more than any other coach. But I felt in my heart that I made the best choice.

Right before my season at Seminole was over, Coach Freeman informed me that she was leaving UI to go coach at Syracuse University. I was disappointed, but as long as Coach Stringer was still at Iowa, my decision remained the same.

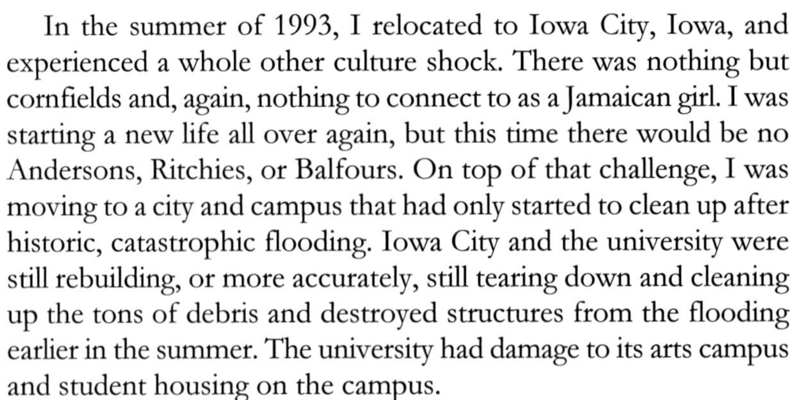

In the summer of 1993, I relocated to Iowa City, Iowa, and experienced a whole other culture shock. There was nothing but cornfields and, again, nothing to connect to as a Jamaican girl. I was starting a new life all over again, but this time there would be no Andersons, Ritchies, or Balfours. On top of that challenge, I was moving to a city and campus that had only started to clean up after historic, catastrophic flooding. Iowa City and the university were still rebuilding, or more accurately, still tearing down and cleaning up the tons of debris and destroyed structures from the flooding earlier in the summer. The university had damage to its arts campus and student housing on the campus.

I moved into Slater Hall, situated where the sports, law, and medicine departments are concentrated. Slater was next door to the UI Fieldhouse – the old gym complex where years earlier the

Hawkeyes had played their basketball games and held their wrestling matches before finally moving competition and practices across campus to the brand-new Carver Hawkeye Arena. The new arena and my classes were on the opposite side of campus from where I was living.

At the bottom of the hill on which Slater Hall stood was the Iowa River, and most of the classes I had were going to be on the east side of the river, while all basketball activities were on the west side. This split in location between classes and practice allowed me the opportunity to become well acquainted with the CAMBUS public transit system, which was funded in part by student fees and provided transport all around campus. Finally, bus stops again. The CAMBUS even dropped students off in downtown Iowa City where shopping and entertainment could be found. With such a huge campus, this was a welcome relief to me.

This campus was much different than Seminole Junior College. Because of its size, the UI campus was like a city in itself. I was grateful that I had Coach Stringer as a role model who I deeply admired for her accomplishments, all achieved as a woman of color.

The Hawkeye women's basketball team had been to the NCAA Final Four the previous spring, and some of those players were back for their senior year. I knew I had to stay focused and determined to better my basketball skills.

In October 1993, practice with Coach Stringer and the Hawkeyes had begun. Basketball training with Coach Stringer was nothing close to what I did in Seminole. I was stunned by the intensity and hours spent and by the physical and mental strain. Her boot camp often led me to wonder if I was entering basketball practice or the military. Starting at 5:30 a.m., we had a three-mile run. I had proven that I was not one to quit after my trainings with Coach Smiley, but Coach Stringer's trainings were at a whole other level. I excelled at long-distance running, even though I'd always been a sprinter, since I walked and ran a lot in Kingston. But I never dreamed of running at 5:30 a.m.

After our three-mile run, we performed basketball suicide drills. We divided into two groups, guards and post players. Since I was a tall post player, most assumed I should run with the other post players, but coach put me with the guards, which meant I had to make a faster time. I felt humbled that she believed I was fast enough to compete with the guards. Although, for that drill, I'd rather compete with a bunch of 100 year olds. For suicide drills, we sprinted from the baseline to the free-throw line, back to the baseline, then to the three-point line, back to the baseline, then to half court, back to the baseline, then to the free-throw line on the other end, back to the baseline, then to the baseline on the other end, and finally, back to the baseline. This drill was timed, and if a player didn't make their time, the whole team had to do it all over again.

Just when I thought suicide drills were the killer, the real culprit of evil, the push-up, reared its ugly head. We had to do 10 push-ups per minute, and I only ended up doing two. I was allergic to push-ups because my arms shook uncontrollably. I started sweating profusely, and some Jamaican curse words would ultimately escape my mouth.

This was after completing only two push-ups.

The final drill was the sit-up test, which wasn't as bad as the push-ups, but sit-ups were still not easy. My feet kept rising with each sit-up, so two team managers had to pin my feet down. I repeatedly apologized to them, as it seemed every other sit-up was accompanied by passing gas. I wished it meant the end of the drill, assuming the team managers would seek relief from such torture. No such luck.

Spring semester started in January in the heart of Iowa's long, awfully harsh winter. The brutal Oklahoma weather was no comparison to the bone-chilling cold of an Iowa winter. There was ice covering the ground with a wind chill below zero. I turned into a popsicle each time I stepped out of my dorm room, although I was covered in clothes from the top of my head to my toes, with only my eyes exposed. It was at that time during an introductory sociology class that I first met Adjunct Professor Mark Chaffee, who was a six-foot-two white hippie. It was a mandatory introductory class that had several hundred students. I thought I could easily go and be invisible.

I had Professor Chaffee's class right after lunch, and often my stomach would not agree with lunch. The school cafeteria only cooked processed foods and my stomach had still not developed the capacity to digest it. Day after day, I would get up from the middle of the large middle section, work my way through my row, leave, use the restroom and come back.

Professor Chaffee noticed my pattern of leaving in the middle of class, from the middle of the section, and then returning. I guess I caught his attention because of my long, lean stature. A few days later, Professor Chaffee asked me to stay after class so he could talk to me. He asked if I was okay and if there was something he could do to make sure my classroom experience worked for me. He told me he thought I often looked a little under duress. I told him my leaving class each day was because the food I ate at lunch often made me ill. I apologized for disrupting class, explaining that I ate lunch right before his class, and about half-way through class, my stomach had fought long enough, and I was forced to excuse myself.

Already skinny, I started losing weight and he inquired about my lean size. I knew that I could not afford to lose weight. I shared that I was indeed having trouble with the unwanted weight loss and that I often felt weak and tired. I had little money, and my troubles with hunger made it hard for me to focus on studying.

Professor Chaffee expressed that he had a background in working with students on issues in their lives, which often meant listening a lot and being an advocate for students in different circumstances. He told me that I was in a fairly unique situation as a foreign student-athlete. He immediately understood how I was not connected to the culture. I explained to him that I had no resources to afford clothing, extra food, and personal hygiene items. He understood how it left me exposed when I had personal issues to wrestle with alone. I didn't have to tell him, as he also seemed to understand about what I was experiencing because of the scholarship bind. After that conversation, Professor Chaffee quickly stepped in as a mentor.

As UI employee, he wasn't allowed to be of any assistance – not class-related or as an alumna of Iowa – because of NCAA rules. The more he thought about it and listened to me, the angrier he got. He so easily saw it – a young, vulnerable, foreign, female athlete, brought to the University of Iowa to compete for the women's basketball program, who had no one to turn to when I needed personal support. He hadn't realized how significantly restricted even my coaches were as to what they could do to help with basic needs.

It felt good that there was a professor who could hear my challenges and understand them more than I could in terms of the bigger picture. He seemed to recognize that my vulnerability was magnified because of the economic situation of being from a family from a small village on a Caribbean island with developing nation status.

Professor Chaffee could put into words the things I felt and tried to express but didn't have all the words at my disposal to explain like he did. He recognized that the NCAA almost assumes that its scholarship students come to a university or college setting able to purchase clothing, food on weekends when the cafeteria closed and personal hygiene supplies. There was no space under those scholarships to cover students who were even poorer than the average poor American student. No special allowances, no special assistance. As a poor student, I was consequently left feeling helpless.

I started going to Professor Chaffee's office to find a quiet study space away from the noisy dorm environment. He explained to me that, had I been a "regular" student and not one enmeshed in the web of regulations created by the scholarship, offering me help would have been simple and easy. He decided that the only thing he could do was to write the appropriate people at the NCAA, carbon copy the appropriate people at UI and wait to see what happened. He asked for my permission to do so, not wanting to endanger my scholarship and because he highly respected the world that Coach Stringer created with her "girls." But watching me lose weight had stretched his tolerance for institutional neglect too far, he said.

He was determined to do more than give support.

Professor Chaffee said he knew and understood all the rules surrounding scholarship athletes. He didn't agree with them all, but he understood what they were trying to protect in terms of how Americans as a society understood amateur sports and how vulnerable and corruptible young athletes might be through money.

I could understand how an athlete with my level of vulnerability could be corrupted to do the wrong things. If money can so easily corrupt adults, the possibility of it corrupting youth is only magnified due to their inexperience and vulnerability. I understood that challenge.

Professor Chaffee was unable to find any relief for me from the NCAA. He gave it his best try but ended up nowhere different than when we started, with everyone's hands tied and with me still isolated and badly needing support.

We traveled to California to play against the University of Southern California (USC) which also included a trip to Universal Studios, courtesy of actor Tom Arnold, a UI alumnus. After a long game with both teams pressuring on defense, it had come down to about 10 seconds remaining on the clock in the final quarter. The game was close, as we trailed by two points. USC was about to shoot a free throw, and I sat on the bench, anxious to get back in the game.

As a new player, I was nervous to ask Coach Stringer to put me in for the final seconds of an intense game that was coming down to the wire. Nevertheless, I yanked her skirt and said, "Put me in coach. I will get the rebound." She looked at me, then looked at the scoreboard. She looked at me again, shook her head, smiled and then directed me to line up at the free throw line. My heart was racing, my adrenaline was pumping and I just couldn't disappoint her.

Coach Stringer was strategic the whole game, but on this play she lined up all her best three-point shooters in positions to get the ball after the rebound. UI six-foot-one forward Nicole Tunsil was my target to pass the ball to after rebounding. USC shot the ball, which bounced off the rim. I grabbed the rebound with less than five seconds on the clock and quickly passed the ball to Nicole as she stood at half-court. The whole crowd stood in silence.

Nicole's three-pointer swooshed into the net just as the buzzer went off, winning the game by one point. The Hawkeyes – exhausted and relieved – swarmed Nicole as the buzzer sounded for the game-winning basket. I was jumping in the air, knowing I was part of our team's success. Coach Stringer embraced me, and I shouted "I did it, coach! I did it! I got the rebound for you!" She grinned and replied, "Yes, you did."

Coach Stringer believed in me with the game on the line, and I believed enough in my rebounding skills. It was an astounding finish to a tense game that was filled with good basketball. I got my first feel of that last-second emotion, and there were no words to describe the adrenaline rush. Just when I thought small things didn't matter, we won the game by a mere one point. Our dramatic victory was ours to take back home to Iowa.

I was having a good practice, so the coaches and a few teammates were giving me compliments. It felt so good because I struggled most days just to remember the plays. Then, one of the seniors I was guarding in practice, who wasn't very happy I was showing her up that day, said in a nasty tone, "Not every day is Christmas, so enjoy this day." I responded, "Well, Merry Christmas!" I then continued playing. I was learning to give as well as get. I would no more just take what bitter people had to hand out. It felt so liberating to stand up for myself.

I had to focus my attention on the big picture. Moving to America to study drove me to want to work to ensure that more children who had a background similar to mine were increasingly afforded great opportunities as well. To build that part of my dream, to give back, it was necessary for me to focus academically while at UI and do well on the court.

I waited patiently for the first basketball season to pass because I knew the following year, I would be a much stronger player. There were so many plays to learn, but I was constantly on the sidelines repeating every movement Coach Stringer taught us so that I could perfect them. There was no way I wasn't going to be a star in Iowa.

CHAPTER 8

NO PAIN, NO GAIN

It was the first semester of my senior year, and I was more prepared psychologically than my previous year. I trained all summer in basketball, making training camp much more bearable. I was in much stronger shape to take on every single test, with the exception of push-ups. I had to do that test twice. I just didn't care for push-ups at all, but I knew I had to pass the test, so I worked on them almost every single day. I talked to my arms constantly, telling them to quit their shaking. But, they didn't listen. This was going to be my playing year. I was more skilled and more confident. I wanted to impress Coach Stringer. In the absence of mommy, she became a mother figure to me.

The practices started off great. I was better with the plays and jumping above the rim every chance I got. The coaches were all impressed with my improvements. Coach Tim Eatman, an African American man encouraged me and helped strengthen my skills.

At the beginning of the basketball season, during one of our practices, I made a turn during a layup and heard a loud pop. I saw the concern on Coach Stringer's face. I felt my right knee give out. When I tried to walk, the pain was excruciating.

I went to the doctor, and he said it was a minor sprain in my medial collateral ligament (MCL) outside the joint of my knee. But, it felt way worse than a minor sprain, since the pain was too intense. The doctor scheduled a minor procedure in two weeks. In the meantime, our athletic trainer helped strengthen my knee muscles to prepare me for the surgery.

On the day of the procedure, the doctor began performing the fairly quick minor surgery on my MCL. Once he started, however, it turned into a major, three-hour operation since, in actuality, I had torn my anterior cruciate ligament (ACL), a major knee injury requiring reconstructive surgery of the ligament in the center of my knee.

I awakened in the hospital alone and crying. The first thing I saw was my fat knee all wrapped up. A nurse came in and offered me some crushed ice for my parched mouth. Although, I would have preferred to have some oxtails with rice and peas and mommy, but neither was available at the time.

I felt overwhelmed because I knew there was a good chance that this type of injury could be career-ending. The doctor came in and told me he had used my patellar tendon to repair the injury and that I was all mended. My prognosis looked good. It depended mainly on my focus and hard work in rehabilitating my injured knee.

Alone in my hospital room, I heard the click-clack sound of shoes walking closer and closer to my door, and the entire coaching staff and a few of my teammates entered. The room was filled with laughter as my teammates joked that now they can beat me down the court since I was always first in the sprints. It felt really good to know they cared.

After they left, I realized I had a long road of recovery ahead, and began to cry. Professor Chaffee walked in and just sat by my bed, holding my hand, letting me cry. It helped to have someone there, someone to affirm for me that I was not alone.

I was discharged from the hospital with crutches and pain medications. Now the hard part. I had to learn to walk again. Instead of being in recovery for just four weeks, as had been discussed for the diagnosed MCL injury, I had to be out for the entire season. I was looking forward to playing in my final season at the University of Iowa, but my knee injury robbed me of that chance, and I was devastated. But, I had to step up, focus, and begin rehabilitation.

The icy winter weather made it difficult to walk with crutches, with the Midwest wind blowing right through me, nearly lifting me up off the ground. Walking on ice without an injury was problematic enough. I slipped sometimes, almost falling to the ground. Nonetheless, my knee hurt more from straining to balance on the ice. The pain medications made me feel drowsy and nauseated, so I tried to tough it out, but that effort was short-lived. The pain from putting repeated stress on my knee while walking on ice was unbearable. The recovery was more painful than the initial injury itself.

On my first day of rehab therapy, the trainer attempted to bend my swollen knee, and I yelled out in about four different languages, none of which I actually spoke. Day after day, I started feeling more defeated and decided that, since I wasn't playing, I shouldn't have to wake up at 4 a.m. for rehab therapy. I despised the pain associated with rehab therapy, and equally despised watching my teammates' 5:30 a.m. practice, longing to be out there with them. I felt helpless and angry because I had worked so hard to get to this point. Injured players were to report to rehab an hour before practice, but I reasoned that bending my knee in rehab therapy was too painful, so I made the decision to skip morning rehab for an afternoon rehab.

After practice, Coach Stringer called me into her office, saying the athletic trainer had contacted her. I sat down, and she said, "You must have lost your mind! You should have come to me before making that decision on your own." I adored Coach Stringer, but her discipline scared the hell out of me, just like my mommy.

Tears filled my eyes because I felt I had disappointed her and, once again, that no one really understood the struggles I was going through. As the tears began to fall, she went into "mama mode." I was overwhelmed about my injury and vented to her about my experiences in Iowa City. She gave me a hug, and I felt such a relief. I needed her belief in me to help me believe enough in myself to keep pushing through. Needless to say, she approved my rehab therapy for afternoons and I never missed another rehab.

Although Coach Stringer wanted me to attend practice so I still felt a part of the team, it deeply hurt to watch my teammates practice. The guilt of not being able to play on the court was overwhelming. I fought back tears each time because sitting out was holding me back from being the talented player I knew I was. Not being able to be on court was the hardest part of my injury, but I certainly didn't miss suicide drills.

As I struggled through mental and physical anguish, I met Margaret Alston, a 30-something African American physical therapist and a doctoral student. Our friendship literally formed out of my pain, our paths crossing at the perfect time. She understood my physical pain and advised me on ways to strengthen my knee and relieve pain in the absence of my athletic trainer. Slowly but surely, she became a mentor and big sister. I told her about my financial struggles, and she opened up her home to me with home-cooked meals, endless advice, and even free hairstyles. Margaret's friendship was God's way of taking care of me. I was now being reminded of where I came from and where I was headed in life, and not focusing on my current circumstances.

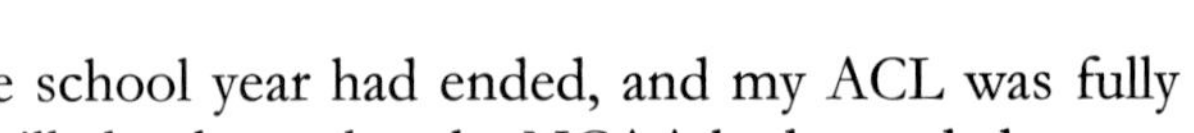

The school year had ended, and my ACL was fully healed. I was thrilled to learn that the NCAA had awarded me medical red-shirt status, which gave me one more year to play basketball under Coach Stringer and continue my education, since I had more courses to complete before graduating.

After our women's basketball banquet, Coach Stringer called an emergency team meeting. Unannounced team meetings were rare. My teammates and I were trying to figure out the reason for the meeting, as everyone was there, and no one knew of anything bad happening to any team member.

As Coach Stringer walked into the locker room, all the chatter stopped instantly. You could've heard a pin drop. She had that presence, especially in this moment of concern we all shared. Her face and voice seemed sad, as she began by stating that we were a great team. She spoke about how difficult it had been after losing her husband who suffered a fatal heart attack on Thanksgiving Day in 1992. Tears filled her eyes, her voice trembled, and she shared with us the most difficult news for all of us.

She told us she was leaving UI, since she had been offered a head coaching job at Rutgers University in New Jersey, and for the sake of her emotions, spirit and family, she needed this change.

The locker room was still silent. I was standing near my teammates, Tiffany Gooden, Nadine Domond, Malikah Willis, Timicha Kirby, Shannon Perry, Tangela Smith and Angela Hamblin, and we were all stunned. Known as the "Sensational Seven," they were All-American top high school basketball players and the top recruiting class in the nation. They had just completed their freshmen year and, like me, came to UI solely for Coach Stringer. For all of us, this unexpected news was a hard pill to swallow.

As hurt as I was, I was even more hurt knowing Coach Stringer's life in Iowa was deeply affected by her husband's death. During the 1992-1993 season, her team was already on a run when it occurred, a run that ended in the finals of the Women's NCAA Basketball Championship. Many things shifted for Coach Stringer in that personal tragedy and its painful memories, all of which led to her decision to leave Iowa. Coach Stringer's extended family was in Pennsylvania, and she felt it was important to her and her three children to be closer to them. I figured her decision wasn't about anything other than her needing to live somewhere she could heal.

Still in the locker room, I pulled my shirt over my face and began to weep. I knew it was a difficult conversation for her, but after hearing about her sudden departure, it was hard to process. I worked so hard to strengthen my knee to come back stronger, only to be hit by this crushing news that Coach Stringer was leaving. This time, there'd be no rehab therapy to help me recover.

I immediately felt panicked about the finality of my basketball dream, hoping to pack my bags and go to with her. I pleaded for her to take me with her, but she didn't have a spot for me on the Rutgers team. I merely hoped to follow a coach whom I considered to be a hero.

I had to face this new chapter without Coach Stringer and tough it out. Although I understood her circumstances, I just wanted her to stay. That was my expectation when I signed with UI. This wasn't just a coach leaving me, she was my mother figure.

Coach Stringer adhered to her plan and left for Rutgers. Walking into the arena without her strong presence left me feeling misplaced. It was tough on the entire team, as her decision to resign made it difficult to adjust. Nothing could have prepared me for the bleakness of what I was feeling. I came to play for a hero of mine, and she walked away. I kept asking myself, how could she do that? But, deep down I understood. Her presence meant so much to my emotional well-being. I learned from her just enough to continue my journey, since she encouraged players to also develop their character – a priceless lesson that stuck with me.

After experiencing a season-ending injury and grueling rehabilitation, my final season as a Hawkeye began. We waited anxiously on the announcement of our new head coach, realizing any new coach would have a challenging morale problem to confront. As soon as our assistant coach, Angie Lee, was promoted to head coach, much to my dismay, Coach Eatman then announced his resignation. Coach Lee had inherited the daunting task of coaching a team whose members primarily came to play in Iowa solely because of Coach Stringer.

About six games into the season, I made a turn attempting a layup during practice, and my right knee suddenly gave out – again. My knee was throbbing in pain as I hopped off the court. The doctor came into the athletic training room to evaluate my knee. He then stated that my knee had rejected my patella tendon, the ligament that attaches the bottom of the kneecap and the top of the shinbone, which happened once in every 10,000 cases. That was nearly a breaking point for me. If I thought my luck couldn't get any worse after the first knee injury and Coach Stringer's departure, I was wrong.

I needed basketball to help me attain my life goals. With either basketball or a college education providing the path, I knew I had to make something work, or I would be going back to Kingston with little to show. Despite feeling so defeated, I was determined to make my last season a resounding success.

While my willpower was in the right direction, I had to sit out another season. That, in itself was unbearable, and I for sure didn't want to go through another surgery, recovery, and rehabilitation.

But I didn't have a choice.

After a successful surgery, rehab therapy started right away. Same routine as before, but an even colder winter. I awoke at 4 a.m. in agonizingly cold weather for rehab therapy, still sliding with my crutches on the ice. I worked hard with the new athletic trainer and within four months, my knee was mostly healed.

During this emotional and physical chaos, my graduation date was approaching. I had struggled emotionally throughout my two years in Seminole and emotionally and physically throughout my years at Iowa, but I managed to make it through. I studied sociology as an undergraduate and felt a sense of accomplishment that I was about to receive my bachelor of science degree. Sociology captured my attention because I had enjoyed studying the group influences on people's behavior and the functioning – as well as the dysfunction – of human societies. I was captivated by the many group and identity dynamics affecting our personal lives, our communities and the global community.

I had come to America already fascinated by different cultural backgrounds. Too many people fear those who are different just because they are different, but I was curious and I wanted to learn more about all these differences. Sociology and psychology had really intrigued me. And now, here I was at the University of Iowa, about to earn my undergraduate degree.

A week before graduation, I was elated when mommy called saying she was coming to the ceremony. Then, I received a letter postmarked from Kingston, Jamaica from daddy. Ever since I'd left Jamaica to come to school in America, he had written me letters. However, this letter started off saying how proud he was of me, and as I continued reading, I was excited to learn that he was also coming to my graduation. For the first time, I would have both of my parents with me at a significant moment in my life. I had never shared any special moment with the three of us together.

For days, I eagerly prepared for their arrival, cleaning the apartment which I shared with two other student athletes. My parents flew in together the day before my graduation and planned to stay for three days. I borrowed a friend's old beat-up car to pick them up from the airport in Cedar Rapids, a larger city than Iowa City, about 30 miles away. I could hardly wait to see them. I hadn't seen daddy in 6 years, and mommy since my graduation in Seminole. I hoped that the car would hold up because it had never been driven so far. I was also very proud that I could show off my driving skills. After all, neither of them had ever seen me drive before.

I drove past the endless Iowa cornfields and, after what seemed like forever, finally reached the airport and parked the car. I made sure that I was early because there was no way for them to contact me if they landed and did not see me. I sat and waited, looking at people greeting their loved ones. Suddenly, I saw mommy and then daddy. I called out to them and rushed to embrace them. I felt like a little child, who sees her parent after the first day of school. It was so wonderful to have them both in Iowa for such an important event for all of us.

The drive back to my apartment seemed much shorter, as daddy questioned me about the car and driving. They were impressed that I learned how to drive and drove so well. I was tickled, being so grown-up and capable of things they'd never seen me do. When we arrived at the apartment, it didn't take long before mommy was in the kitchen cooking curry chicken. She had brought some Jamaican seasonings and snacks for me. Mommy sent me out to the grocery store for additional items, and when I returned, daddy had straightened my room. I had some books and paperwork out, and he put everything neatly away. His gesture was thoughtful, but I didn't know where anything was.

After dinner, they showered and retired to bed. Daddy slept in my room, and mommy was given my roommate's room. The only thing is, I forgot to disclose to mommy that my roommate's bed was a water bed. It was her first introduction to a water bed, and she hollered after she failed miserably to roll out of the bed. We all laughed. Needless to say, she switched rooms with daddy. And, he hardly slept worrying all night that the bed would burst.

The next day was graduation day, and I awoke to a Jamaican breakfast of fried dumplings with ackee and salt fish. Mommy ironed all of my clothes with no wrinkle spared. Daddy dressed in a suit and tie, and mommy wore a floral dress. I was proud to show off my cap and gown. We arrived on campus for the graduation ceremonies. Professor Chaffee met us outside and was more than excited to meet my parents. They all seemed so proud of me.

As the graduation began, I kept looking around for them among the thousands of people. Sitting with the expectant graduates, I waited anxiously for my name to be called so I could hear my parents shouting. When they finally called my name, my heart started beating fast. I looked into the crowd and saw my parents waving and cheering. I waved back, smiling ear to ear.

After graduation, I found my parents, and mommy gave me the same kiss and hug as she had at my previous graduation in Seminole. Daddy appeared to be seven feet tall as he stood there so proud. He had just witnessed his first child graduate from college. I felt so accomplished and so humbled that I had been able to achieve success in my parents' eyes, to witness a milestone important and significant enough for them to leave Kingston and fly to Hawkeye country, see my world in Iowa and beam with pride.

CHAPTER 9

PUT ME IN COACH

Much to my disbelief, the NCAA awarded me a sixth year to play basketball after suffering two season-ending knee injuries. Because of my earlier medical red-shirt status, coupled with how late in the season we were when I was reinjured, I was uncertain whether I'd be awarded a second red-shirt. I was able to play during the 1996-97 season as a first-year graduate student, studying sports psychology. My second knee injury made me skittish to get back to playing, so I needed to get my strength and confidence back.

During the summer of 1996, I learned from Professor Chaffee that when a designated group wasn't scheduled to use the UI Fieldhouse gym on a weekend morning, he played basketball with a team of men ranging in age from 30 to 40. I went over to watch them and figured their level of playing the game might be good for me to compete against to rebuild my confidence. The gym opened at 8 a.m., and they played sometimes until 11a.m. I felt the draw. I wanted to play, and no women were a part of their morning games until I came. So, I had to prove I belonged there.

When the guys were first learning of my skill level and capacity, one of the players on an opposing team went up for a jump shot over me, thinking he could make an easy soft jumper. I chased him into the air on defense, reaching for the sky and batting his shot away, with a triumphant, "Git that crap outta here!" None of them had played against a woman before who could grab the basketball rim. I was taller than most of the men on the court, and they learned something about me fairly quickly. I could jump.

We trash talked, but mostly everyone joked around while playing, something that was very refreshing. Ultimately, I earned my place on the team. The guys on the court respected my game, and playing with them helped me strengthen my knee and rebuild my confidence.

In fall 1996, I started grad school to pursue a master's degree in sports psychology after missing back-to-back seasons due to injuries. After a second bout of intense rehab, I was ready to give basketball all I had. This was going to be my last year playing for UI after being red-shirted twice. Everything was on the line this year, and I was very conscious of that.

As tough as pre-season basketball training was, I was in great shape, since these guards were much quicker, so the suicide drills didn't last too long. I knew this was going to be the year for me to finally shine.

I was now the team co-captain, voted in by my peers, and was ready to work with the players and the new head coach, to make this season a big success for all of us. We were all familiar with Coach Lee, and I believed she'd give me a fair shot with playing time.

But I was wrong.

I was no longer consumed by rehab therapy and was now able to fully contribute to the team. I felt misunderstood by Coach Lee. My final year, my time to shine, but I was given very limited playing time, and I didn't know why. I couldn't figure out how to do right by her, and perhaps she couldn't figure me out – or didn't care to. It seemed like no matter how hard I tried, I just couldn't connect with Coach Lee, and I was growing more and more frustrated.

I'd already been challenged enough with two seasons out on a blown knee. This was more anguish than I was prepared for. Even though things had changed, I wanted to give Coach Lee the same work ethic that I gave Coach Stringer, and I felt strongly that I did. When I played, I averaged 4.3 rebounds, 7.1 points per game, and made more than 56 percent of my shots. I was certain my statistics would increase if only I could play consistently. I felt like she was playing mind games with me. I worked hard in practice. I was giving everything I had. It felt as if Coach Lee went out of her way to make it hard for me, and I struggled to the point of depression. I had so much to lose with my unpredictable future after leaving Iowa.

Regardless of court time, the Hawkeye fans still gave me all their love and support. Before and after games, I interacted with fans as if everything was going well. The whole situation was tearing me apart. At one level, the fan support was comforting and at another level, I felt like their support forced me to wear a mask that hid the rage that was weighing me down. Fans inquired about my lack of playing time. It took everything within me to hold it together, not because of a bad game or a bad loss or a sports injury, but because of minimal opportunity to make visible my value to potential scouts for the American Basketball League (ABL), a professional basketball league for women. This was yet another authority figure who, for unknown reasons, was trying to keep me from fulfilling my dreams.

I had so much anger and disgust with a coach, who seemingly had no regard for me being under her care. I felt the absolute powerlessness of being not just a student-athlete, but a poor, foreign student with no way to solve this troubling situation. Basketball was not only tough on the body but also on the spirit.

The anticipation and excitement I felt at the beginning my final season – the crowning season of all my sacrifice and dreaming – was now being pulled from my grasp by a new authority figure over whom I had no impact. Seeing my dream reachable in which I'd placed so much effort and time and now, with every game minimally played, I slowly watched my dreams deferred.

I was mentally and spiritually exhausted.

But I had high hopes for our final home game, which was the senior game. In the final home game, senior players started the game even if they weren't normally starters. What an unbelievably wonderful gift, when I discovered that mommy was coming to watch me play in the senior game. In all the years I'd played basketball, mommy had never seen me play. Not once. The most important thing I ever wanted in this torturous process was for mommy to see me play basketball. Now, more than ever, since my future in basketball seemed unpromising.

With thousands of fans in the bleachers at Carver Hawkeye Arena, all I could hear were two Caribbean accents. Mommy was sitting next to my teammate Nadine's mother, and both were shouting "DEFENSE!" The only thing was that we were on offense. For the entire game, they cheered louder than the school's cheerleaders. Nadine came in her freshmen year as the number one point guard recruit in the country. We bonded like sisters since we both had Caribbean roots.

It was so humbling, so healing, so beautifully surreal having mommy there. She had been my lifelong inspiration, and I figured this was probably the first and last time she would ever see me play. I never told her about all the obstacles in Iowa. I never told her much about the pain and rehab therapy and early practices. She knew very little of my struggles since first being offered a path to success through basketball because I didn't want to burden her with worries about which she could do nothing. And now, after all the times I could have used her words of encouragement, her embrace to help soothe my soul, she was finally here.

Of all my years of playing, this moment with mommy cheering me on was the most special.

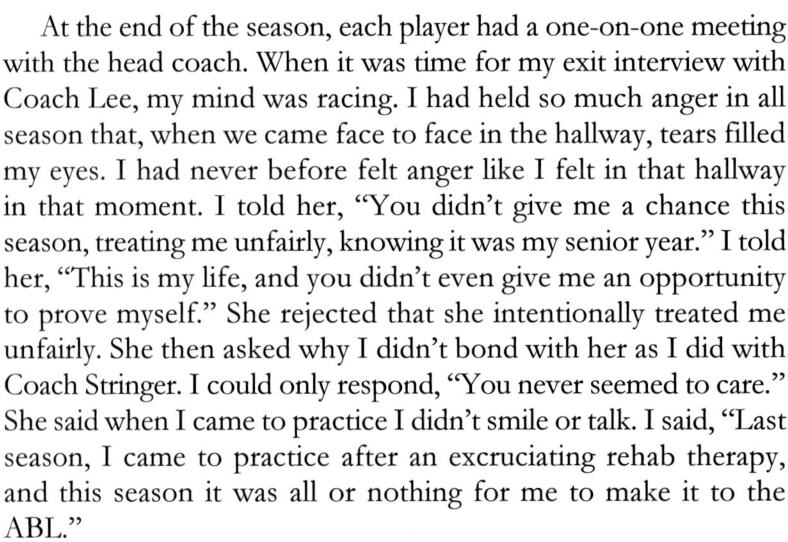

At the end of the season, each player had a one-on-one meeting with the head coach. When it was time for my exit interview with Coach Lee, my mind was racing. I had held so much anger in all season that, when we came face to face in the hallway, tears filled my eyes. I had never before felt anger like I felt in that hallway in that moment. I told her, "You didn't give me a chance this season, treating me unfairly, knowing it was my senior year." I told her, "This is my life, and you didn't even give me an opportunity to prove myself." She rejected that she intentionally treated me unfairly. She then asked why I didn't bond with her as I did with Coach Stringer. I could only respond, "You never seemed to care." She said when I came to practice I didn't smile or talk. I said, "Last season, I came to practice after an excruciating rehab therapy, and this season it was all or nothing for me to make it to the ABL."

I stood there in disbelief with her invalid reason. I was so upset with her for her stance on treating me as she did, which seemed to point to no outcome other than to ruin my chances of getting into the ABL. I played too infrequently, which prevented ABL scouts from assessing my skills and whether there would be ongoing knee problems. I bluntly shouted to her that she was selfish and inconsiderate and that she drained my confidence and energy so much that I hated the game for the first time in my life.

Standing in the hallway, releasing pent-up emotions, our voices got louder and louder. She motioned for us to talk inside the stairway so as not to bring attention to our commotion. It was the first time I had raised my voice to a coach and she didn't want us to create a scene.

I looked up at her as I stood at the bottom of the stairway, feeling defeated and stranded in my own fear of not knowing what was next for me. This was the end of our shared road, and I didn't think, in that moment, that she realized or cared that I had no hope for my future. I needed her to hear my anger and pain as much as I needed her to understand me before we veered off in different directions.

"Did I work hard?" I shouted to her.

"You worked harder than everyone, and that was never the problem," she responded.

"So, because I didn't smile or talk at 4:30 in the morning, is that the reason you have an issue with me? Now it's too late because no scouts know who I am or what I'm capable of because you took me not smiling as personal about not liking you. It was never about you. You made it about you. All I wanted was to play hard for you and to get the opportunity to be scouted." She stared at me, silent for a few seconds, and then admitted that she was wrong in her approach and apologized for her treatment of me, saying that she didn't think about the affect it had on me. And, I apologized for raising my voice.

At the end of the emotional interview, we hugged each other and shed more tears. I felt hopeless, unable to see where to go from there. She then extended an olive branch and said that when I finished grad school, she would try to get an agent to help me secure a job playing professional basketball in Europe.

I felt as though my future in basketball was dim because opportunity had been so close, and yet I had been denied access. I could have done so much more for the program my final season. I just wanted to feel that she saw me as a good enough athlete and believed in me.

After smoothing things over with Coach Lee, one of my professors decided to act on her stance that athletes didn't deserve scholarships. In class, she voiced her disgust with the whole athletic scholarship system. It was as if she thought athletes were getting free education without earning our keep. Starting with my first injury to Coach Stringer's exit, to Coach Lee's non-smiling vendetta, I just couldn't seem to catch a break in Hawkeye land.

The pain I endured in both mind and body was clear evidence that student-athletes earned their keep. The lifetime scars on my knee spoke clearly to the sacrifice of our bodies. My torturous last year spoke to the sacrifice of our emotions and our hearts.

Poor American students received assistance from the federal government, but since I was a foreigner in Iowa City on a student visa, I wasn't privileged to receive any of that help. I had to constantly remind myself that I was on a mission and I couldn't return to Jamaica without making my family and supporters proud. Now I focused on proving that biased professor wrong.

I had a 50-page final paper for her class, which was a very demanding requirement of length and depth. I worked with her teaching assistant as my tutor, and prepared to write about ACL injuries, a topic with which I had a lot of familiarity. However, the professor strongly suggested that I write about another topic instead of ACL injuries. She stated that it would fit me best as a Black athlete to write about why Black athletes are kept out of the decision-making positions, like quarterbacks in football and point guards in basketball. But, it was totally unrelated to what I wanted to write about. She believed that since I was a Black athlete it would be a fitting topic for me. Yet here was my professor, thinking her "Black athlete" should write about stereotypes of Black athletes. I responded that I had already begun research on my chosen topic, academically and through my own experiences as an injured and scarred athlete, so I wanted to write about ACL injuries and their impact on female basketball players. I knew I had the liberty to choose my topic and had some expertise in the subject matter since I went through my ordeal.

She then gave me the approval, even though she thought her suggested topic was far more interesting. Although it was interesting, I was more interested in finding more information that could be used to help other athletes like me.

When I completed my final paper, my tutor proofread it for grammatical errors, then submitted the first draft to the professor for feedback. To my surprise, my tutor shared with me that my professor asked her who wrote the paper, and she told her that I had. With the professor insisting the paper must have been plagiarized since it was an A-plus paper, my tutor then responded that I worked hard on researching and writing the paper and that she had merely proofread it.

It saddened me that the professor had clear stereotypes of Black student-athletes that made her conclude that I wasn't smart enough to write an A-plus paper. The professor made me feel as though I didn't belong in grad school. She had no idea that I was already struggling with so many other obstacles. I was at her mercy, since the paper was 50 percent of my final grade.

It was the end of my first year of grad school, and I was anxious to receive my "A-plus paper" and final grades. Much to my dismay, I was stunned that the professor actually had given me a C on my final paper. My tutor shared the same disbelief. I was learning more and more not to be silent in the face of abusive authority, so I went to the dean to complain about the professor denying me of an earned grade. However, he advised me that my professor had already left for the summer, and there wasn't anything he could do at the moment until she returned to campus.

Every step of the way, it seemed that I had to claw and hammer at this life process to make it work for me. I was disappointed to tears, because I worked so hard on my final paper, only for my professor to assume that my paper was too good to be mine. It was so enraging and impactful that she could abuse her power, get away with making some arbitrary decision about my work with no proof of any wrongdoing whatsoever and rob me of receiving credit where credit was due. Even worse, there was nothing I could do. It was her way of telling me that, as far as she was concerned, I didn't deserve an A-plus, making her statement loud and clear.

It was my first real taste of some of the -isms that one person might use to disempower another for whom they carry such sickening stereotypes. I already felt different because of my height and being a foreigner, but no one ever made me feel less than they were based on some other characteristic of identity until this experience.

I ended my first year of grad school feeling crushed in defeat and discriminated against. Entering grad school, I had chosen a career goal to become a sports psychologist. My experiences in Seminole and Iowa City had informed me of a lot of the needs that college athletes had for good mental health resources during their competitive years. Such resources were important to not only address the isolation student-athletes, such as myself, had to confront, but also peak-performance issues that kept athletes from performing at their best in given circumstances.

Since my sports scholarship had run its course, I went to meet with my student counselor, Taunya Tinsley, to discuss finishing grad school. Taunya was a young Black woman, who always helped me stay focused on achieving my academic goals as a student athlete. She informed I needed approximately $25,000 to complete my last year of grad school As I was sitting there listening to her, I only had a small amount of savings to my name. I knew that since I was an international student, I didn't qualify for grants and federal loans, so this was out of Taunya's hands. And, it seemed certainly out of mine. I felt hopeless because now even my dream of being drafted into the ABL wasn't even a possibility.

I was mentally exhausted.

My two options were to find a job to provide me with a work permit to allow me to stay in America, or return to Gola. I was so distraught because I thought I did everything right for the American dream – working hard in basketball and in academics to earn my scholarship. My hopes of professional basketball and sports psychology both seemed impossible. I'd come so close, but since the first knee injury, it seemed like so many things had gone so completely wrong. Fighting such a long struggle was overwhelming. I knew I had to prepare for life after Iowa, but I didn't know where to start. I stood out because I was different, which made me hurt far too often. I realized that my place at UI had come to a bittersweet end.

CHAPTER 10

WHEN PREPARATION MEETS OPPORTUNITY

In May 1997, as I was preparing to depart from Iowa City, some of my fellow players at UI mentioned reading an article in the newspaper about a new league called the Women's National Basketball Association (WNBA) which was established in 1996 but making moves to get started. The National Basketball Association (NBA), in an effort to bring some equality to women's sports at the professional level, founded the WNBA. The news piqued my interest.

I never lost contact with Coach Stringer after she left UI and darted off to call her to find out what she knew about the WNBA. She told me the extent of what she knew, and we hung up with her commitment to gather more information. When she called me back the next day, she told me that she discovered that the New York Liberty, one of eight franchises in the WNBA, was holding a two-day tryout in New York City in one week. I was excited and saw it as an opportunity to get into the WNBA. Coincidentally, mommy was visiting her friend in Brooklyn, New York, so I knew I had a place to stay during tryouts. I had been packing to return to Kingston, and now I was preparing to go to New York.

I knew I had to be impressive to stand out from hundreds of other basketball players. This was my chance to prove myself. Suddenly, there again was possibility. The weekend tryouts were Saturday and Sunday, and it was two days before the tryouts. I left my belongings in Iowa City, and Professor Chaffee drove me to the bus station. The bus took me from Iowa City to Chicago, where I then caught a flight to New York. I used my meager savings to pay for this promising trip.

When I arrived at JFK airport, I hailed a cab to the address where mommy was staying. I had been traveling all day and couldn't wait to see her. When I got to the house, I knocked on the door, and mommy opened it, anticipating my arrival. I saw the excitement on her face. She told me she was proud of how I had saved my money, as little as it was. It felt so good to be reunited with her.

On the Saturday morning of the New York Liberty tryouts, I was uneasy, not only because of the tryouts but also because I had to take the ferry across the East River, which I wasn't anticipating. The last time I took a ferry was in Kingston at 7 years old and got extremely sea sick.

Coach Stringer was still coaching at Rutgers, which meant she wasn't far from where the tryouts were being held. I called her, and she said she would come to support me, but couldn't come until day two. They were making cuts each day, so I was even more determined to push myself to the limit to ensure I was present on the second and final day of tryouts.

As I walked up to the ferry, I started to panic as I saw it rocking and the water hitting against it. This is not good. I feared I'd get sick before the tryouts. I took some deep breaths and stepped onto the ferry. As soon as the boat rocked, I rushed to the restroom, ending up sick for the entire ride.

By the time the ferry docked, I had barely enough energy to walk off. I felt as if all my strength was gone, and my head felt dizzy. This could not be happening on the first day of tryouts. I knew there was nothing to do but pull myself together. "Mental over physical," I kept repeating to myself.

I arrived at the College of Staten Island's gym at 8 a.m., carrying a gym bag over my shoulder that contained my knee brace, basketball shoes, and snacks prepared by mommy. Three hundred other women were scattered inside and outside of the gym. It was incredible seeing so many determined athletes. I watched as players who were familiar with each other join forces, while I searched among the scattered athletes to see if there was anyone I knew. I didn't have any basketball associates there, so I just sat inside on the floor to eat a snack since I still felt so low on energy. Although I was weak from my unsettling ferry ride, I also felt light, which was good because whenever I felt light, I could always jump higher. I was relieved that there were not many tall women present, which meant I stood out.

I dozed off and awoke to a loud whistle. Then a voice on a microphone asked all the participants to come inside the gym to listen for their names and groups so that we all could change into the New York Liberty practice jerseys and be grouped accordingly. I quickly got up, and grabbed my bag to join the crowd. I was a nervous wreck.

The New York Liberty's newly appointed coach was Nancy Darsch, who had been the head women's basketball coach for Ohio State University (OSU). She was the winningest women's coach in OSU history, and was an assistant on the gold-medal-winning Olympic teams in 1984 and 1996. I noticed her walking in my direction. She then came over to me and said, "Simone Edwards, your skills impressed me at Iowa. I will be keeping my eyes on you." UI played against OSU twice a year, and she recognized me. I was in disbelief that someone who could have a role in helping me build my future in basketball had seen me play in Iowa after all.

The WNBA Inaugural draft occurred prior to tryouts, so some of the New York Liberty drafted players attended the tryouts to weigh in. I knew I had to leave it all on the floor in order to gain the New York Liberty's interest.

Another whistle blew. To the front of the group stepped Carol Blazejowski, Olympic team member and Basketball Hall of Famer. She introduced herself as the New York Liberty's vice president and general manager. "Welcome to the tryouts for the New York Liberty of the WNBA," she said. She paused, and then added, "I never thought I'd see this day."

She then introduced Coach Darsch, who instructed each group to disburse to one of the three courts in use for the tryout. Neither of them mentioned how many players they were looking to sign, but it was obvious it wasn't many based on the number of draft picks. I wanted to be a part of the team and longed to be one of the players chosen in the final selection.

Once I joined my group, I put on my knee brace which I wore because I wasn't mentally ready to go without one. I hadn't played enough on my knee last season at UI, and I didn't want to take any chances. In hopes that they wouldn't be concerned about my knee injuries or the fact that I wore a brace, my goal was to ensure I shifted their eyes away from my knees and toward my athleticism, which was my dominant strength.

I inhaled and exhaled slowly, trying to control my heart from racing out of excitement and nervousness. I knew I had to play as if I was fighting for my future because, truthfully, I was. As the whistle blew for my group to play against another, I consciously decided to be the standout player on my team. I reflected on my days as a sprinting champion, then began running the court like a deer across an open field. Each and every time the ball went up, I made sure I caught it from above the rim. I could hear the crowd yelling for me to dunk it and loud gasps as I went up above the rim, to knock the ball off the rim. This was my opportunity to show how athletic I was.

At 8 p.m., the coaches posted a list of the 29 players who would be invited back on Sunday. My heart raced as I rushed to look for my name. I saw my name and smiled from ear to ear, as my efforts on day one were enough to be invited back. I was so eager to tell mommy about my first day of tryouts that I didn't feel as bad on the ferry ride back.

Saturday was intense, so I was certain Sunday would be harder work with only the top players remaining. I arrived to tryouts on Sunday morning to find out that the New York Liberty would choose three players. I was so sore and tired from going hard the first day, and once again the ferry ride took a toll on my system. Yet, I was just as determined to make the team, no matter what challenges came my way.

Shortly after I got there, Coach Stringer arrived, and I ran to her and gave her a hug. She asked how my knees were holding up. With her presence, I felt even more focused and confident, like I could take on the world. She was like a boxing trainer in the corner of the ring, and having my trainer come up to my face to remind me how talented I was, made me feel as if I could move mountains.

With fewer people on the court, it was even more anxiety-provoking, but I knew I had to do all I could to make sure there was more attention on my skills. I noticed that some of the players who already had been drafted to the New York Liberty team were there to observe, and I kept repeating to myself that they were my future teammates. I knew if they liked my skills that could better my chances of making the team.

My knee was a bit swollen from the day before, so I took some painkillers to ease the soreness. But then an adrenalin rush kicked in, and I didn't feel pain. I hustled after every ball. I was playing defense on the guards and blocking shots. I was getting all the rebounds and outrunning players down the court for layups. I knew if I was able to get a rebound after a missed shot, it would give my team a second chance to score. I was secure in my skills and strength, and I wanted everyone in that gym to know about them, too.

Coach Stringer observed how much I had learned and improved since she went to Rutgers. I wanted her to be proud of the athlete I had become. My teammates in the tryout group kept saying that I was going to make the team because I was way too athletic not to. I knew my height was an advantage, but I also knew that I had to show that I was the most athletic post-player in the gym. It was such a boost in confidence to have Coach Stringer there to watch me fight for a spot on the team.

Coach Darsch carefully observed my every move during the drills. Everything I did on the first day, I did twice as much on day two. I ran faster and jumped higher. I knew the life I dreamed of living, and the things I dreamed of accomplishing. My whole future was now dependent upon this one critical day.

I had flashbacks of every coach who had ever coached me. I mentally went back to the drawing board by tapping into all the basketball techniques I had learned and stored in my head. I re-evaluated what I needed to adjust and what I needed to improve. This effort on this day would be all or nothing.

Was my all enough?

GM Blazejowski cut Sunday's tryouts short. She called the players together, thanked everyone, and announced she would post a list of the 10 players who had made another cut. From that list, six names would be sent to the league office on Monday. As we awaited the list, they proceeded to take photos of us and obtained phone numbers from each player.

Finally, the list was posted.

My heart was racing. I felt fairly confident about the tryouts after the drafted players had shared that they were impressed with my ability to sprint the floor and by their excited reactions to my blocks and rebounds. I eyed the short list and saw "Simone Edwards." I was encouraged, yet nervous, that the whole trajectory of my life would change as I now awaited a single phone call.

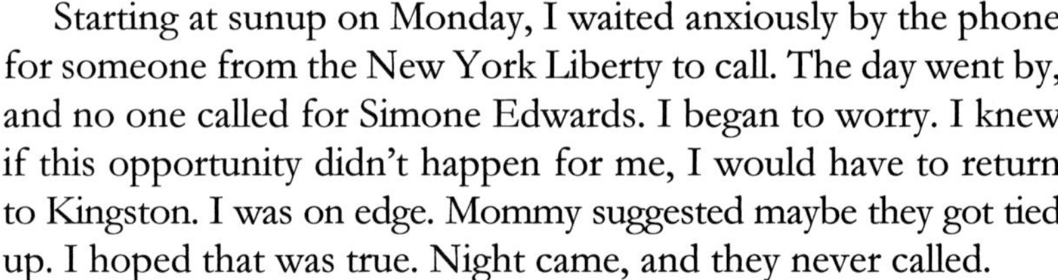

Starting at sunup on Monday, I waited anxiously by the phone for someone from the New York Liberty to call. The day went by, and no one called for Simone Edwards. I began to worry. I knew if this opportunity didn't happen for me, I would have to return to Kingston. I was on edge. Mommy suggested maybe they got tied up. I hoped that was true. Night came, and they never called.

The next day, I awoke at 6 a.m. and waited by the phone. Each time the phone rang, I answered on the first ring. At noon, mommy forced me to step away from the phone to get something to eat. I was driving myself crazy. The moment I was about to lose hope, the phone rang. I reluctantly answered the phone, "Hello?" The voice on the other end asked to speak to Simone Edwards. "This is Simone," I calmly replied, trying to hide my excitement. "This is Carol Blazejowski, the New York Liberty's vice president and general manager, calling to let you know we have chosen you to be a part of the New York Liberty as a developmental player."

I felt as if my heart was going to jump through my chest. I was speechless. I was in shock. I felt as if my whole body was frozen.

"Are you there?" she said.

"Yes, I'm here!" I excitedly responded.

"Are you excited?" she asked.

"Excited? That is an understatement. Thank you so much!" I shouted into the phone.

"We'll overnight you a package to fly you in for training," she concluded.

One phone call literally changed my life. It all felt like a dream. This was the growing women's sports movement, the WNBA, and I was going to be a part of it. Mommy heard me screaming, and she knew it was the call. We both were excited, and I started jumping up and down as we celebrated. "God is good," she said, as she held her hands in the air praising God. I could see the relief in her eyes.

For now, I didn't have to worry for the foreseeable future. At this moment, I celebrated a major accomplishment in my life. A ray of hope. A sport that I considered walking away from so many times finally paid off – except for one, minor obstacle – training camp. GM Blazejowski informed me that for the next month, I would have to successfully navigate through training camp since they would make final cuts of two developmental players prior to the first game. Until then, I would still be trying out before I could finally exhale and see my dream turn into a reality. Nonetheless, all the hard work, dedication, and determination during my time in Kingston, Seminole, and Iowa City had new meaning and purpose.

Training camp and practice were set to start in three days, so I bought a one-way airline ticket to Chicago to return to Iowa to finish packing and say my goodbyes. I was exhausted, and my turnaround time was too short to take the bus. I needed a ride from the airport in Chicago, so I called Professor Chaffee.

"Professor Chaffee, can you please pick me up from Chicago? I asked. He responded, "No, I can't come pick you up, Simone. The airport is four hours away, and I'd have to rent a car." After pleading about 10 times, he finally agreed to come pick me up at the Southwest Airlines terminal at Chicago O'Hare International Airport.

When I arrived, there was no sign of him. So, after an hour went by, I called him from the terminal. "Hi, Professor Chaffee, I've landed. Where are you?" I asked. He responded, "I don't see the Southwest Airlines terminal at O'Hare." I responded, "Oh, I just realized…." He then cut me off, and asked "Oh, you just realized what, Simone?" I hesitantly answered, "Well, I just looked up at the sign, and I'm actually at Chicago Midway International Airport." He shouted, "Simone! I just drove over 200 miles in afternoon rush-hour traffic to O'Hare, and now you're telling me that I have to jump back in rush-hour to drive another 30 miles to Midway?" He sounded quite frustrated. "I'm sorry, Professor Chaffee. I got mixed up," I said.

But he wasn't finished venting. "And, I just hit a guardrail!" he shouted. He sounded a bit stressed, and rightfully so. He finally arrived to Midway, an hour later. He was quiet and seemingly frustrated, so I assumed this may not be a good time to share my good news. But, I tried anyway. I asked, "Professor Chaffee, do you want to hear about my New York Liberty tryouts?" Although he didn't respond, he did, however, make it a point to show me his right fender bender on the driver's side. I took the hint, and figured it wasn't a good time to tell him about the tryouts. This celebratory trip back to Iowa wasn't turning out like I had envisioned.

Around midnight, with less than an hour left to get back to Iowa City, Professor Chaffee pulled over at a rest stop. "Simone, drive," he said. I thought to myself, at least he was talking to me, as he wanted to get some shut eye in the back seat.

The road was more pitch-black than Gola at night, and after a measly five minutes behind the wheel, a huge deer came bounding onto Interstate 80. Just when I thought the night couldn't get any worse, there was a loud thump. I screamed, and Professor Chaffee jolted back up into a seated position, looked out the front windshield and then out the back, as I sat there in shock.

"What happened?" he asked.

"I hit a deer," I responded.

"So, pull over," he said.

I pulled off to the side of the interstate, with Professor Chaffee repeating that his rental car did not have extended insurance. We assessed the new damage, which was way worse than his earlier fender bender, since the deer hit the same fender scraped on the guardrail. This new damage meant that the guardrail's scrape was now minimal, compared to the passenger door and rear fender both deeply crushed with the missing mirror.

Professor Chaffee gave me the same death stare as mommy. He shouted, "Over 20 years, I had a perfect driving record until this trip!" He then paused and calmly added, "Simone, I know that you had no control over the deer sprinting out onto the highway." He then drove the remainder of the trip.

Instead of celebrating my triumph with my favorite professor, a deer was dead, and a rental car was a damaged. Needless to say, as my chapter was coming to a close in Iowa, I literally went out with a bang!

CHAPTER 11

FRUITS OF MY LABOR

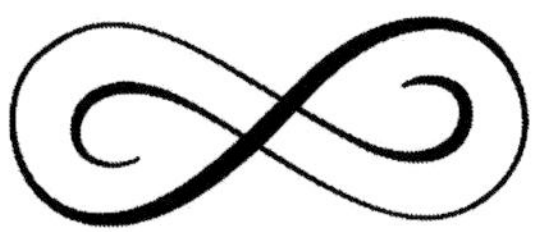

As I prepared to return to New York City, to my surprise, I had a first-class ticket, courtesy of the New York Liberty. My first-time, first-class experience was a red-carpet welcome to the Big Apple. As I stepped onto the plane, the flight attendant escorted me to my seat. She waited as I put my things down and returned holding a tray of orange juice, champagne, and club soda. "Would you like a mimosa or maybe club soda with lime?" she asked. Since I didn't drink alcohol, I enjoyed an unlimited supply of orange juice.

As I was getting settled in a comfortable leather seat with my long legs stretched out, another flight attendant came by to prepare me for the five-course meal. I thought to myself, I could definitely get used to this. It was a dream come true. Literally and metaphorically, I was flying.

When I landed, a tall, regal man stood near baggage claim holding a sign with my name written on it. I waited to see if anyone else was walking up to him, but no one did, so I walked over and asked if he was with the New York Liberty. He said yes. I felt like a celebrity as he took my luggage, whisked me outside to a black Lincoln Town Car, and opened the door. Onlookers stared as I proudly entered the car.

I arrived at my new living quarters, a fancy Manhattan hotel suite, where I was welcomed by a friendly concierge, who helped me out of the town car and into the hotel. The lobby was glamorous with glitzy chandeliers and polished marble floors. My room was located on the 15th floor with amazing views overlooking Madison Square Garden. The room had a gorgeous decor with a massive king-sized bed, huge television, high ceilings and the bathroom was equally spectacular with marble everywhere and frosted glass doors. It was absolute luxury.

I plopped down on the heavenly bed and smiled from gratitude as I felt free from so much darkness. Out of nowhere, I yelled, "Welcome to NYC baby!" I looked through my welcome package, which was a gift basket with fruits, snacks, pins, keychains, and t-shirts, along with our five-day orientation schedule. In New York City, at the threshold of my dream, with little roster space for developmental players, my focus was to not get waived during training camp.

I decided to take a walk around the area. As I opened my door, Rebecca Lobo, a 24 year old, six-foot-four marquee player for the New York Liberty was exiting her room just a few doors down. Rebecca played at the University of Connecticut and on the gold-medal-winning U.S. team in the 1996 Summer Olympics. I excitedly spoke to her as we both entered the elevator, and she warmly said, "Welcome to the team, Simone. How was your flight?" I responded, "Thanks, Rebecca! The flight was great." The elevator stopped on the first floor, and we went our separate ways as I departed to explore the Big Apple.

After walking about six blocks from my hotel, it suddenly dawned on me that not one person spoke or smiled back. For most of the walk, I followed the aroma of roasted peanuts, which reminded me of street vendors that sold them back home in Kingston, pushing their carts shouting, "Peanuts!" I tried without much success to squeeze past people on the crowded sidewalk, mistakenly bumping into a New Yorker, who gave me a dirty look. Nonetheless, I exhaled and tilted my head back in a skyward gaze mesmerized by the lights of Time Square, which revealed the magic of the city. I relished watching different cultures as I was now in a city that was a cultural melting pot. But, most importantly, I learned the basic rules of how to and how not to walk in New York.

The next morning, Sunday, May 25, 1997, was the first orientation day. We held our first official team meeting at Madison Square Garden (MSG), the World's Most Famous Arena. I entered MSG with a great deal of respect, and got goose bumps all over. I followed our guide, and as I entered the locker room, the most surreal moment was seeing my name on a locker. The biggest smile took over my face. I started having flashbacks of my childhood days when my feet were bleeding from running in the streets barefoot. Countless times I walked home after hours of training in the scorching sun as I learned this game that had brought me to this very moment inside MSG. I was in New York City for the inaugural season of the WNBA. I was so humbled after surviving such a tedious journey.

As our meeting began, Coach Darsch asked each of us players to introduce ourselves. As each player spoke, it was apparent that everyone was collectively thrilled and grateful to be a part of WNBA history. After introductions, we collected our practice gear, toured MSG, and it finally started to settle in that this wasn't a dream anymore. We then had a team brunch, followed by a tour of New York City in a double-decker bus. Complete strangers, now teammates, bonded within hours.

Our first week of orientation included all eight of the inaugural season WNBA teams: Charlotte Sting, Cleveland Rockers, Houston Comets, Los Angeles Sparks, Phoenix Mercury, Sacramento Monarchs, Utah Starzz and New York Liberty. I sat next to 34 year old Cynthia Cooper, who signed with the Houston Comets. I had never heard of her before, but learned that the five-foot-ten player was a member of the 1988 gold-medal-winning U.S. Olympic Women's Basketball Team. I was immersed in the moment of being among some of the best players in the world.

The "long-foot gal" from Kingston, Jamaica was among greatness. It made me feel so proud to know that I was one of the chosen few because of my hard work and skills. I felt most proud to represent my country and the Caribbean at this important liftoff in professional women's sports. This wasn't college anymore. I was no longer juggling classes or trying to find my place in life. I was now a professional athlete.

Running practice drills at the Reebok Sports Club gym was tough. It was all or nothing for the next three weeks at training camp, as coaches evaluated me daily on the court. These players were so competitive, so motivated. Quickly, I learned what brought my teammates to share this court with me and with each other.

Teresa "Spoon" Weatherspoon was a 32 year old point guard and the most fun teammate because of her outgoing personality. She was a natural leader in the way she communicated with teammates. Spoon wore her hair in cornrows and only stood at about five-foot-eight, but she was a beast on the court. She was fast with the ball and a very aggressive defender. She was warm and constantly encouraged me throughout the practices, although I was just a developmental player, which meant I had to be activated to play in the games. Rebecca "Becca" Lobo, who played center, was able to use her right and left hands equally well when it came to dribbling and shooting the basketball. I was still trying to figure out how to get my left hand to effectively hold a fork near my mouth. Becca was gracefully humble, even though it seemed that every second the media was in her face, shouting questions and demanding answers.

Kym Hampton was a 35 year old center and real team player. She was drafted as the number four pick in the 1997 WNBA Elite draft and another beast to be reckoned with on the court. Kym, with her motherly spirit, offered compliments whenever I performed well on court, even if it was against her. She stood six-foot-two with a larger physique, so my lanky frame would often bounce off her as she knocked me out of her way going up for a layup. I worked hard for those compliments in an effort to not be slung across the court. Vickie "VJ" Johnson was a 25 year old shooting guard who stood five-foot-nine. VJ laughed as she knocked down a short jumper or took another player to the basket.

Sue Wicks was a 30 year old, six-foot-three forward. She was the craftiest, dirtiest player, but also one of the biggest hustlers on the team. There was hardly a time that any player would get a rebound or a loose ball without Sue there fighting with you for it. Rhonda Blades, a five-foot-seven brunette guard, was like the Energizer Bunny since it seemed she never got tired. She would compete hard the entire practice, never letting down. Sophia Witherspoon, a five-foot-ten guard with a short blonde afro, was a great scorer and three-point shooter on court, who preferred to wear jersey number 13, declaring it was an outcast number for many. Trena

Trice was a six-foot-two solid post player, who played basketball overseas for nearly a decade before the inaugural season. Kisha Ford was a five-foot-ten guard-forward who played college basketball at Georgia Tech, where she was the all-time leading scorer in team history. Cassandra Crumpton was a five-foot-ten guard developmental player, who was impressive shooting the ball from the three-point line. Diana Vines was a 29 year old, five-foot-eight guard-forward developmental player and single mother who played overseas. Jasmina "Jazz" Perazic-Gipe was a six-foot guard-forward in the middle of her prime and my biggest fan as a teammate. The mother and wife participated in two Olympic Games and competed professionally overseas. She mentioned that she thought that I was chosen for the active roster after watching me at the tryouts and, coming from a talented player like her, I was honored.

All of my teammates showed me so much support. Even though I was a developmental player and not on the official roster, they still helped me continue to learn and hone my skills.

The end of the intense training camp had come, and I continued to improve with each practice, competing against other centers. I knew the time to cut one more player was near. I convinced myself that I did not make it this far to not become a part of this team.

The final decision was made to waive Diana Vines and, as bad as I felt for her with the chemistry that had formed between the players, I was relieved that it wasn't me. All the times I was not considered talented enough, fast enough, tough enough, big enough or in any other way worthy of a chance, I was now proud of the fact that I had made history as the first Jamaican *and* first Caribbean WNBA player.

The first-ever WNBA game was the New York Liberty playing against the Los Angeles Sparks on June 21, 1997 in Los Angeles. Since I was a developmental player, I didn't travel with the team on away games, but watched the nationally televised game in my hotel suite. Before a crowd of more than 14,000, the first points were scored by Los Angeles Sparks guard Penny Toler, but the Liberty ultimately defeated the Sparks, 67-57 at the Forum.

After winning two more away games, our first home game was on June 29, 1997, and the Liberty was scheduled to play the Phoenix Mercury at MSG. Mommy was determined to not miss my first WNBA game, and I knew I would be moved by her presence. I was equally proud of simply being part of history, even if I was just bolstering the bench.

When I walked onto the court at MSG I was still in awe that I was now a part of the team. My mind kept going back to that tall, clumsy, awkward, poor girl from Kingston, who was taunted for her size, lankiness, and big feet. I had flashbacks of trying to fit in with the boys in Kingston to prove my skills on the court and of the bully girls taunting me at that first practice with Coach Smiley. There were so many memories replaying in my head.

Consequently, that moment for the first WNBA game in New York City started hitting my hidden and unknown expectations of the world almost immediately. It was very emotional, and I was conscious of how far I had come. I also was becoming increasingly more aware of how far women had come – in my lifetime and in mommy's lifetime. I was deeply aware still of how I was witnessing the fruits of a long struggle for social change.

As I sat on the bench, my enthusiasm could not be contained. I was motivated to cheer with the crowd at courtside, never having dreamed of getting the chance to be in such a moment, close enough to watch. At the end of the bench, I was riling up the crowd, excitedly urging the crowd to cheer, stomp or clap. Then, I heard my name coming from familiar voices, as mommy yelled, "Go, Simone!" Next to her, was Professor Chaffee proudly waving his hand. I might not have been on the court, but they were equally proud of the role I played for the Liberty. From the opportunity to engage and entertain the lively fans, to talking with Spike Lee, accompanied by his young daughter, to now being a part of the story of this inaugural season, it was all very humbling. Meanwhile, on this exciting ground-breaking day in New York City in front of an MSG crowd of more than 17,000, we defeated the Phoenix Mercury, 65-57 in our first home game.

At the end of the game, despite my being a developmental player, I was swarmed by fans for autographs and pictures. They enjoyed my antics swaying to music with my big smile and rhythmic motions at the end of the bench. Such avid fan support coming in my direction kept me pumped and nourished, while I was not even playing.

After the game, I joined mommy and Professor Chaffee, who was in town on business. Like mommy, he didn't want to miss being a part of this historical moment. I was so grateful for them to share this amazing experience with me. We all went out to dinner afterwards to talk about the game. Mommy was thrilled by the reaction of the crowd toward me as I raised my hands, urging them to cheer louder. She was proud that I was a part of something so significant. She reminded me of how neither of us initially knew what the game was, but I promised her I was going to be good at it. She reminded me that I needed to keep working hard so that one day I would be on the court like the other active players. "I promise you, mommy, you will see me play," I said as I hugged her and rested my head on her shoulder. I may not have played a minute on the court, but I was determined that the Liberty's fan base would know who I was. No matter what my role in the inaugural season, I gave it my all.

We won our first seven games before losing to the Phoenix Mercury. Our team ended the inaugural season with a record of 17 wins and 11 losses, qualifying as one of four teams for the postseason in the eight-team league. It was only a single-elimination tournament advancing the Liberty to the first-ever WNBA Championship game.

Since we made it to the championship against the Houston Comets, I could finally travel with the team. My teammates were excited to have me on the road with them, and I was excited to be with them as a participant, of sorts, in the first WNBA final. Readying for the sellout crowd of over 16,000, we knew the Comets team was tough. They had Cynthia Cooper, the player I sat next to during the players' orientation, who averaged 22 points per game; shooting guard-forward Sheryl Swoopes, the first player to be signed in the WNBA; and Tina Thompson, a very skilled post player.

The New York Liberty played hard, but the Comets claimed the victory, defeating the Liberty, 65-51. The loss was devastating to our team. At the same time, we finished second place in the conference and were proud to be there for this historic first. In so many ways, as a part of the path to building my dreams, it was a perfect season for me. I wanted so much to be out there on the court, but that would be another step in my path.

CHAPTER 12

A STAR IS BORN

Coach Lee, my former coach from the University of Iowa, fulfilled her promise of finding me an agent. So, I received a call from an agent, named Tony, who told me Coach Lee had given him my phone number. He informed me that he could get me a contract in Israel to play basketball. Most WNBA players played overseas during off-season to continue to improve their game and earn more money. He sent me the contract, and I signed with the Elitzur Ramla team in Ramla, Israel, which was a predominately Jewish city in central Israel, between Jerusalem and Tel Aviv.

Mommy was concerned about the violence and turmoil in Israel, but I was just glad to accept a well-paying contract. This was my next step in earning a comfortable living playing basketball, helping my family and building the rest of my dreams. In September 1997, during my first off-season with the Liberty, I traveled to Israel to improve my game.

As the plane took off, it suddenly hit me that I had no idea what to expect once I arrived in Israel. I had only had one introductory phone call with the Israeli coach, and my agent handled everything else. In spite of that, I was nothing but relieved to not have to financially struggle anymore. I could not wait to start my next adventure.

After a ten-hour flight, I finally arrived in Ramla, and my coach, Ilan Kowalsky, who spoke fluent English, whisked me off to get a physical. The doctor had me run on the treadmill for a few minutes, tested my blood pressure, heart rate and knees, and then advised Coach Kowalsky that I passed the physical. Following the physical, we drove straight to practice, wasting no time. When I walked into practice, I met with the trainer, a burly Israeli whose English-speaking skills were nonexistent. He kept his go-to ice spray, which I soon realized he used for every injury. I prayed to God that I never had an eye injury.

Coach Kowalsky introduced me to the team. We started practice to prepare for our first game in October. My first practice with my new team was going well, as curious observers voiced their amazement of a WNBA player's athletic abilities and skills, which hyped me up to show off a bit. After practice, I met the players individually in the locker room. Although the primary language was Hebrew, most of my new teammates spoke broken English. The locker room was quite different than the WNBA or even college, primarily because the locker room didn't have any lockers. It reminded me of my humble beginnings, where even an inside gym was not a part of my expectations.

After practice, Coach Kowalsky drove me to my new apartment, where I was paired with my new teammate, Lashawn Brown. Lashawn was a six-foot-five post player, who previously played for Louisiana Tech. Neither of us had a car in our contracts, so our teammates took turns taking us to and from practice. One of our teammates, Yamit Aspir, picked us up mostly. Yamit was an Israeli, who lived outside of Ramla. She wanted to improve her English, so spending time with me was beneficial to her. In exchange, she taught me Hebrew, but I did a bad job at learning the language. Most importantly, I got all of the curse words down.

Some of my teammates spoke about Ramla's negative public image and its neglect. I, however, never felt threatened or uncomfortable walking around the city despite the dangers that surrounded the country. The people were warm to me, and I was fascinated by the beautiful blend of ancient and modern Israel, which featured historical landmarks, such as the White Tower, standing six stories high, with a spiral staircase. Streets were fragrant with captivating smells of exotic foods from the outdoor market and vibrant with the sounds of conversations held in multiple languages.

During practice, a few days before our first game, I was jumping for a shot, which triggered my left knee to forcefully twist. I couldn't believe I just hurt my good knee. The team doctor revealed that I had a slight meniscus ligament tear, which was a tear in the cartilage of the knee. I had been through two ACL surgeries on my right knee, learned how to walk again not once but twice, and now this. I was disappointed because I was just getting started.

The surgeon advised me to have surgery, but the only thing I heard was him saying that another option to strengthen my left knee was by playing in a brace. That was my glimpse of hope. I wasn't ready for my season to be over before it even got started. I was completely over surgeries and the horribly long and painful rehab, so I decided to strengthen my knee on my own, using our trainer's go-to ice spray, and wearing two knee braces throughout the season. I chose to have surgery at the end of the season. For once, a team was relying on me to help them win a championship, and I had to prove myself. It was unfamiliar yet exhilarating to finally be part of a team that believed I could contribute right away. So, I opted to play.

Our team was extremely talented. We had a mixture of Israelis, Eastern Europeans, and others who played as foreigners. My nemesis on the team was a Russian player named Luda, who I clashed with on the court almost every practice. She was the nastiest player I had ever played with. I learned all of my Russian curse words because of her, since she shouted expletives each time she hit me with her elbows. She made it clear that she wasn't fond of me coming in as a new post-player, since that had been her position, and taking the attention she had been getting. What she failed to realize was that this Jamaican knew how to throw elbows with hurricane-like force. It wasn't long before she discovered I wasn't one to back down from her forceful physical play. I wasn't about to play nice while she played dirty.

The first game of the season with Elitzur Ramla had come. I was so pumped. My knees were wrapped in tape, and over the tape I wore my knee braces. Ramla was known for its women's basketball team, so the die-hard fans filled the small gym shouting, singing, and blowing horns. It was an overwhelming feeling.

During the game, I was scoring and rebounding up and down the court. Fans were chanting, "See-Mone Ed-Wards" louder and louder. To hear fans chant my name for the first-time ever was an unbelievable feeling. It was so loud in the gym that at times I couldn't even hear the referee's whistle. I was one of the top scorers, while leading the game in rebounds, and we won our first game. For the first time, I felt validated as a professional player.

After the game, fans rushed to the court to celebrate our win. Due to language barriers, I couldn't understand them, but I felt their excitement for the win, and that was good enough for me.

Our team advanced through the playoffs, and I made my mark as the league's most dominant rebounder and one of the top scorers. Our team won the Israeli Championship but lost the Israeli Cup. Ramla had won a championship before, so the team and fans were disappointed to lose what would have been their first Israeli Cup. Even though I had a strong game, it wasn't enough to take us to a victory.

At the end of the season in the spring of 1998, I signed on with a new agent, Oded Avni. He had spoken to me during the finals of the championship game after we were introduced by one of my teammates. Elitzur Ramla wanted to re-sign me for the next season, but they weren't paying me in a timely manner. I didn't want to worry about whether I'd be paid on time, so that swayed my decision to play for another team. Oded succeeded in getting me signed to a new team, Bnei Yehuda, located in Tel Aviv, right before I had my minor knee surgery performed for the meniscus tear in Israel.

Three weeks later, I returned to New York for training camp with the Liberty. I was disappointed that I didn't make the Liberty's roster, but I didn't realize I had probably caused more damage to my knee and hurt my chance of returning to the WNBA by not having surgery earlier. At this point, my knee needed weeks to get back into a competitive-ready state, and the WNBA season only lasted for a few months. I walked away from the Liberty knowing I had to live with my decisions. But, I felt a bit indebted to play for the Elitzur Ramla coach and management, who shared with me that they depended on me to get the team to the championship. That also fed my ego. So, I opted to play.

I now had to wait for another WNBA opportunity the next year. Elitzur Ramla covered my costs to rehab my knee during the summer. It was a long, painful summer of regret, but one more lesson learned – the hard way.

By October 1998, I was fully recovered. I headed to Israel to join the Bnei Yehuda basketball team. I arrived in Bnei Yehuda, a suburb of Tel Aviv. My new coach was Eli Rabi who believed in my abilities to lead the team, and it didn't take long to realize that he was an effective basketball coach. His coaching style was an extension of his personality, and although he was a shouter, he was one of the most easy-going people I've ever been around. I enjoyed playing for him and the club. I was also thrilled to rejoin my good friend and former teammate from UI, Nadine Domond, as my teammate in Bnei Yehuda. Nadine was still a jokester, and we played well together. She went over and beyond to show off her dribbling skills on court, always trying to embarrass the opponent guarding her. Coach Rabi repeatedly shouted to her to keep it simple, but that wasn't her game. It was showtime whenever Nadine was on court.

That season, we helped advance Bnei Yehuda to the playoffs for the first time in the team's history. Although we were unable to win the championship, the fans were just as passionate as Elitzur Ramla's when it came to cheering for their team. I had a solid relationship with the team and the city, and my paychecks were always on time.

After the season in Bnei Yehuda, I traveled back to New York to learn that I got an offer to play for the WNBA's Detroit Shock from their general manager and head coach, Nancy Lieberman. However, the excitement was short-lived because the offer fell through since it was past the deadline to sign foreign players. Coach Lieberman didn't realize I was still on a U.S. work permit. I was crushed because I anticipated not only returning to the WNBA but also playing for Coach Lieberman, who was regarded as one of the greatest figures in American women's basketball.

I returned to Bnei Yehuda in October 1999 to play for Coach Rabi again. During a regular season game, right before the playoffs, an opponent stepped on my foot and it was badly sprained. I could barely walk, resulting in me being taken to an acupuncturist who worked on my foot as we prepared for the playoffs. I didn't practice leading up to the playoffs so that my foot could fully heal.

When the playoffs began, I wrapped my swollen foot, took some painkillers and averaged a double-double each game. Our team made the Israeli Cup finals, but lost. The loss hurt more than my foot did because I really wanted another championship. Nevertheless, my stats were high, averaging 22.5 points and 11 rebounds. It was my best season in Israel, despite the foot injury.

My contract allowed me an extra airline ticket that I could use for myself or for someone else, and I used it for mommy. So, she visited with me near the end of the season. Since she was a devout Christian, Israel was a country she had dreamed of visiting. When she arrived in Bnei Yehuda, she was surprised that Israel was so modernized. We whisked off to Jerusalem to see the sacred site of the Wailing Wall, an ancient limestone holy wall where believers come from all over the world to pray. We then went to The Garden Tomb, known in the Bible as the site of the burial and resurrection of Jesus. She deeply enjoyed this tour of sacred antiquity.

Our next tour stop was the Dead Sea, appropriately named because its high mineral content allows nothing to live in its waters. With its unusually high salt concentration, it is said that people could easily float and not sink in the Dead Sea, however, mommy and I chose not to test that theory. Instead, we sat in the sand as the water washed over our feet, and then mommy covered herself with its famous mineral-rich black mud. There were a few people already way out in the sea floating, and we didn't see anyone sink, so obviously, the theory was true.

I was ready to reenter the WNBA. This time I was determined to make a team on an active roster. Oded partnered with an American agent, Mike Cound, so Mike worked on trying to get me back into the WNBA. In the meantime, I parted ways with Bnei Yehuda in 2000 after being offered more money and a car to play for the underdog Maccabi Ramat-Chen team, for the next season in Tel Aviv. Meanwhile, as my game had greatly improved in terms of overall skill, I received interest from the Miami Sol, New York Liberty, and Seattle Storm WNBA teams. I was excited and looking to rebuild my path into the WNBA.

I flew back to the States at the end of April, and a few days later I was in Miami for a weekend tryout for the Miami Sol. Then, I headed to the New York Liberty training camp, where it had all started for me professionally. Although, the inherent pressure of tryouts was daunting, this time around I was more confident and developed as a player.

A day after my Liberty camp, I received a call from Mike saying I was going to Seattle. The Seattle Storm got first pick over the Miami Sol and the New York Liberty, because they were a newly developed team in the WNBA and, consequently, they had first grabs at me.

I was thrilled that all these teams were interested in me, but even more excited to be a part of another inaugural team. Seattle was to be my new home, and I felt blessed for the opportunity.

CHAPTER 13

RISE OF THE JAMAICAN HURRICANE

In May 2000, I arrived in Seattle to prepare for training camp at the Sonics & Storm Training Facility. Being that it was the Storm's inaugural season, I was once again making history being part of their first team roster. I was officially on a WNBA active roster. For sentimental reasons, I chose #4 on my uniform, representing mommy's four children. It was like a rebirth returning to the WNBA, and I went in with confidence, knowing that I was a very solid, leading player because of my overseas experience. Now I was signed, having had a central role in winning championships overseas as one of the top rebounders in the world.

Linn Dunn was the Storm's head coach and general manager, and our three assistant coaches were Missy Bequette, Kathy Anderson, and Gary Kloppenburg. Coach Dunn was a Tennessean with a warm personality and strong southern accent. She coached at Purdue University in the Midwest at the same time that I played at UI, so she was familiar with my game. The inaugural Storm team was comprised of players I wasn't familiar with or hadn't played against before. The Storm chose six-foot-four forward-center Kamila "Vodka" Vodičková as its first-draft pick of the franchise. She was from the Czech Republic, and we were the only two foreign players on the team. She was set up as the centerpiece of the offense, with five-foot-eight guard Edna Campbell as the outside imposing threat.

Coach Dunn was not very subtle when it came to cutting players during training camp. Players would be practicing on the court, shooting around or just conversing, and as soon as Coach Dunn entered the gym, it was as if you could suddenly hear everyone's heartbeat, especially the rookies.

There were two main courts and eight extra basketball rims, which came down from the ceiling, for four on each court. Players were usually pretty spread out. Coach Dunn would walk to wherever a player was standing on the court to inform her that she was waived. I never heard what she told them, but from the looks on their faces, I wondered if it was something like, "Hey, you. Yes, you. Your lifelong dream ends right here, right now." But, afterwards you'd hear a sigh of relief across the gym from those not cut. We all dreaded the entrance of Coach Dunn. Some players were so nervous, you could see the fear in their eyes.

During another practice while we were shooting, waiting for practice to begin, one of the weaker players in camp was standing next to me. As luck would have it, Coach Dunn walked over toward us. Everyone stopped to look our way, eyebrows raised.

I felt confident in my skills, and Coach Dunn told me that I was her best shadow, which was the person at the top of her press defense, scaring the heck out of opposing players who dared to have the ball. The teammate next to me looked as if she was going to crap her pants. I, too, was a bit uncomfortable because there was nothing guaranteeing me a spot on the Storm. I told the frightened player not to worry, but even I didn't believe that. That was the longest walk ever. I didn't know if I should offer her a last cigarette or what. Given the awkwardness of the situation and hating to witness women wailing over broken dreams, before Coach Dunn could reach us, I shot the ball in a manner that it missed the rim so badly, I would be required to run after it. I decided that if it was me Coach Dunn was coming to waive, she would just have had to catch me.

"Simone!" Coach Dunn was loudly calling my name. I pretended that I didn't hear her, since my heart was beating out my chest. Then Coach Dunn called my name even louder in a manner that made it possible for the entire gym to hear. My heart started beating faster and I was all shaky-kneed, preparing for the slow death of being cut as I walked toward her. "Yes, coach?" I said. "Simone, we are going to go over the pressing defense today, and

I need you to always be on the ball," Coach Dunn said rather plainly and matter-of-factly. She believed in me and my defensive game, and I took pride in that. Although she had nearly given me a heart attack, I calmly answered, "OK, coach." She then walked over to the other post player and promptly cut her. During training camp, this was a job we had to fight to keep literally every day.

Our first regular season game, we lost to the three-time defending champion Houston Comets, 77-47. After starting off the season 0-4, we secured our first-ever victory with a 67-62 win over the Charlotte Sting. As the season progressed, we achieved our first-ever win at KeyArena with an intense 69-59 overtime victory over the Los Angeles Sparks. The team finished the season, winning only six games with a 6-26 record after a 79-46 loss to the Sacramento Monarchs. I finished the season as the team leader in rebounds and second in scoring, playing in 29 games with my strong defense, rebounding, and speed running the court, but only averaged 7.4 points and 4 rebounds.

Even with a gloomy start, I knew Seattle would be my home. Storm fans were nothing short of amazing because our thousands of die-hard fans kept coming out every game despite our low record, still cheering us on until the final whistle.

It was the beginning of the Storm's second season in May 2001, and the Storm landed 19 year old, Australian six-foot-five center Lauren Jackson as the number one overall draft pick.

I don't recall a time when Coach Dunn ever shouted at Lauren, the star on the team. It was as if Lauren had an invisible barrier around her that prevented Coach Dunn from shouting at her; however, she had no problem shouting at me. During one game, while I was sitting on the bench recovering from some really intense outpouring of energy, Lauren performed a bad play on court. Now, without an invisible barrier, I expected to hear Coach Dunn shout, "LAUREN!" But no, we all heard Coach Dunn instead shout "SIMONE!" I knew she wasn't telling me to "get in the game." So, I just shouted back, "I am on the bench coach!" My teammates all started laughing. Coach Dunn called my name so much, I could hear her calling my name in my sleep and was considering seeking a support group for the constant ringing in my ears of her voice. Nevertheless, Coach Dunn was one of the best defensive coaches I knew. I became a better defensive player being coached by her. She was tough on me, but it pushed me to get better and improve my skill set. She mastered teaching defense, which meant we practiced defense for hours until my feet felt as if they were on fire. I lost two toe nails in the process.

Lauren entered the WNBA known as the Australian player who infamously yanked off Lisa Leslie's ponytail and threw it on the floor during the 2000 Olympics game. There was going to be no truce anytime soon between Lauren and Lisa. Because of the hair debacle, these two marquee players were sworn enemies in the league. Lauren was unapologetic on court, if you were playing against her. As a result, the first game we played against the Los Angeles Sparks, we expected Lisa to go hard for Lauren as payback. However, Lauren and I switched on defensive assignments, resulting in me guarding Lisa instead without Lisa realizing it. Out of nowhere, I caught a strong elbow to my ribs. Then, Lisa turned around and said, "Are you okay? I'm sorry Simone, I didn't realize it was you." Although I had had my share of elbows to the ribs, I had involuntarily taken a hit for Lauren.

The 2001 season progressed with an 83-70 victory over the Phoenix Mercury, with the 83 points setting a franchise record. The very next game, rookie guard Semeka Randall scored a career-high and franchise record of 28 points in a 70-63 victory over the Orlando Miracle. The victory marked the first time that the Storm won two consecutive games. Consequently, the Storm fell to the Washington Mystics 72-69, during in the first quadruple overtime game in WNBA history.

The Storm's first game in New York against my former team was in July 2001. I was so anxious to return to Madison Square Garden. Even more so, I was not a benchwarmer, and mommy, Aunt Novelette and her son Chain, and my sisters Juddeth and Venece were coming to see me play. I was pumped on game day as I went through pre-game warm-ups, taking in the atmosphere. MSG was not the friendliest of places to play for an opposing team in terms of fans booing. After a competitive game, the Liberty ended up defeating the Storm, 67-53.

After our post-game briefing, my sisters ran toward me, over the moon with excitement. I thought their excitement was for me, but they revealed they weren't leaving my side until they met their favorite player Teresa "Spoon" Weatherspoon, who just become the first WNBA player to reach the 1,000 point mark. For some outlandish reason, I assumed I was their favorite player. Since they at least expressed how proud they were of me, I called Spoon over to meet them. With her approachable personality, Spoon was such a good sport with my giddy, star-struck sisters. We may have lost the game, but that night my family was part of the journey of my life. That, in itself, was a victory to me.

Next, the Storm defeated the four-time WNBA champion Houston Comets for the first time in franchise history, 72-55. Yet, our season ended as the Storm fell to the Monarchs 72-62 in the season finale, finishing the Storm's second WNBA season with a 10-22 record, four games better than the previous season. I finished behind Lauren in rebounds and was third in points behind Lauren and Semeka. Even though we only won 10 games, I ended the season as the Storm's all-time leader in games played and minutes, and earning a franchise record 14 rebounds versus Orlando. This season's boost gave us optimism about our team's future, as I deeply felt that our team would continue to be strengthened by recruiting talented players and improving our game.

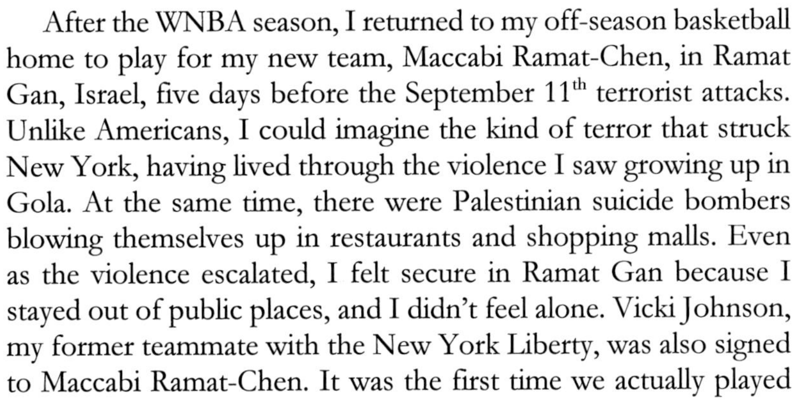

After the WNBA season, I returned to my off-season basketball home to play for my new team, Maccabi Ramat-Chen, in Ramat Gan, Israel, five days before the September 11th terrorist attacks. Unlike Americans, I could imagine the kind of terror that struck New York, having lived through the violence I saw growing up in Gola. At the same time, there were Palestinian suicide bombers blowing themselves up in restaurants and shopping malls. Even as the violence escalated, I felt secure in Ramat Gan because I stayed out of public places, and I didn't feel alone. Vicki Johnson, my former teammate with the New York Liberty, was also signed to Maccabi Ramat-Chen. It was the first time we actually played together during a game, since I was unable to play as a developmental player with the Liberty in 1997.

I was a regular at The Seafood Market after games, a restaurant and after-hours disco barely 10 minutes from my home. After one particular game, I broke my ritual and decided to cook at home that night. I was shocked to learn that my rare absence spared me from multiple suicide bombings around The Seafood Market.

Ramat Gan resembled a chaos in paradise, reminding me of Jamaica with its sandy beaches coupled with violence. Sounds of laughter and locals playing "matcot," a Middle Eastern version of table tennis without the table, were background noises while playing beach volleyball in the warm sun. I had developed friendships with my Maccabi Ramat-Chen teammates, so I shuffled between different families, always at meal time, savoring the native cuisine. They ensured that I partake in the local Israeli dishes. I discovered the universal connection of music with Shirli Zafri, an aspiring singer who was looking for someone to help her write songs in English. I thought it would be challenging to try such a thing because I had written songs and poems as a teenager with my sister Juddeth. Shirli came from a musical family being that her mom and dad were a singing group. On my days off from playing basketball, we met to listen to her melodies. I was blown away by her voice. We collaborated, and I wrote two songs for her, which she performed live in Europe. My Hebrew improved, and I felt as if Israel had become my second home to Jamaica, surpassing how I felt about living in the States.

But, after all those years of learning to survive with so little and yearning to live a life comparable to Beverly Hills back home, when I finally had the ability to live comfortably, material things no longer impressed me. I didn't feel pulled to buy expensive possessions. My worth had never been tied to what I wore or what I had, and there appeared to be no good reason to suddenly shift direction and tie myself to such things.

I recognized that I had reached a point where I could begin to work on the next chapter of my dreams, the dreams regarding the children impacted by poverty. I chose to help others who lived very much like I had when I was a child in the poverty-stricken outskirts of Kingston. This effort to help lift children's dreams was part of my commitment to myself and my neighborhood since I first stepped away from Gola. I knew what it was like to live in the prison of poverty, to have even the bare necessities, like shoes to protect your feet. I knew what it was to dream of a way out, wanting without any hope or direction.

To start working on this part of my dream, I established a charity called Simone4Children, and donated half my earnings toward education, clothing and food for children in Kingston. My struggles as a child, both in poverty and especially dealing with bullying by children and adults calling me names because I was different than them, added fuel to propel me toward the success I was aiming for in helping vulnerable children. Once more, I found a way to step up and build this opportunity to help, something I'd dreamed of for many years.

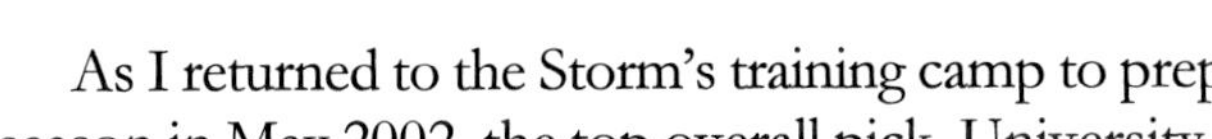

As I returned to the Storm's training camp to prepare for another season in May 2002, the top overall pick, University of Connecticut (UConn) five-foot-nine point guard Sue Bird, joined the team. She was coming off an undefeated season at UConn, winning two NCAA titles. She was not accustomed to losing.

Lauren was barely dealing with our frequent losses. She wasn't used to losing either, and I don't think any of us on the team had lost that many games in a season before playing in Seattle. It was mentally and physically draining for every single player. At training camp, players from the inaugural season dwindled. We now had two marquee players, Sue and Lauren, who didn't seem to immediately bond. Lauren had been the star of the team, and then Sue stepped in from the draft, and the media was swarming around Sue. It took a few games before they started bonding off the court and creating chemistry on the court. Once they finally connected outside of the game, they became a dynamic on-court combination. Sue's ability to dominate plays and Lauren's scoring abilities brought the team greater hope and higher expectations.

In the season opener, Sue made an impressive debut, scoring 18 points and dishing out six assists. However, we lost to the Liberty, 78-61, with Lauren injured with a sprained ankle. The next game, the

Storm captured our first win of the season against Portland, 57-47. That game started a three-game winning streak for the Storm.

When the Storm played the Utah Starzz, Polish seven-foot-two center Margo Dydek was my least favorite player to guard, outsizing Shaquille O'Neal as the tallest professional female basketball player in the world. With a seven-foot reach like a dragon wing, she held the record for most blocks in the WNBA. At six-foot-four, even I was short standing next to her. Too busy looking up instead of down, the referees constantly missed fouls against her while on defense, when she'd trip me with her knees if I attempted to drive pass her to the basket.

During one particular home game, I knew I had to prepare for Margo. Despite all my efforts, she kept blocking my shots. She stood under the basket as I took a shot from the free-throw line, and she still blocked my shot. I did a reverse layup, cleared after passing her, and then – "BAM!" – out of nowhere, she blocked me again. Did she block me from over the rim? It was frustrating and embarrassing. I couldn't go out like that. I knew I had to block her at least once during the game to redeem my dignity. I was substituted out of the game for a few minutes and used that opportunity to watch and study her slow-motion turnaround shot. At seven-foot-two, she didn't have to jump. There was no need to. When I got back in the game, my main focus was to block her shot all the way to Poland, since the last ball she blocked on me was probably lying on the beach in Jamaica. Her team came down on offense and passed her the ball in the middle of the paint, between the basket and the free-throw line. Margo confidently turned around to shoot. By then I was hyped because as she was about to shoot, I rose like a hurricane and blocked her shot. The Storm crowd cheered, and I was excited. She looked shocked. My job was done.

Speaking to reporters after the game, I blurted out, "If our team is the Seattle Storm, then I am the Jamaican Hurricane." I was still up to my old habits, entertaining fans with my dancing on the sideline, during the pregame or whenever I was sitting on the bench, encouraging them to stand and cheer when the team needed a boost. One of the things I enjoyed most of all in my self-appointed fan development role was performing my infamous shimmy-shake with Doppler, our team's mascot. Doppler, a maroon-furred creature with a cup anemometer on its head, and I had a special bond at the game, entertaining fans together on court.

Doppler and I worked so well together as a team that during one game, I was on the opposite side of the court from Doppler, down on the baseline with the ball, and the opposing team came to double me up on defense. None of my teammates were making themselves available for me to pass them the ball outside of the trap. Running against the clock, in the heat of the moment, I mistakenly passed the ball to Doppler, and the entire sold-out KeyArena crowd burst into laughter, including me. In my peripheral vision, he was the only one in uniform who was open. He did a phenomenal job in catching the ball. Unfortunately, Doppler's catch didn't count.

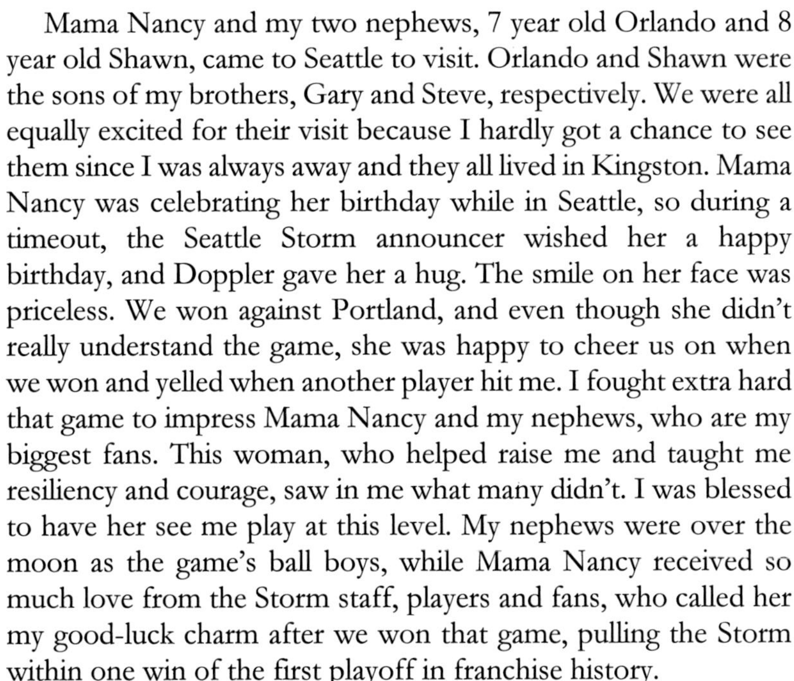

Mama Nancy and my two nephews, 7 year old Orlando and 8 year old Shawn, came to Seattle to visit. Orlando and Shawn were the sons of my brothers, Gary and Steve, respectively. We were all equally excited for their visit because I hardly got a chance to see them since I was always away and they all lived in Kingston. Mama Nancy was celebrating her birthday while in Seattle, so during a timeout, the Seattle Storm announcer wished her a happy birthday, and Doppler gave her a hug. The smile on her face was priceless. We won against Portland, and even though she didn't really understand the game, she was happy to cheer us on when we won and yelled when another player hit me. I fought extra hard that game to impress Mama Nancy and my nephews, who are my biggest fans. This woman, who helped raise me and taught me resiliency and courage, saw in me what many didn't. I was blessed to have her see me play at this level. My nephews were over the moon as the game's ball boys, while Mama Nancy received so much love from the Storm staff, players and fans, who called her my good-luck charm after we won that game, pulling the Storm within one win of the first playoff in franchise history.

We finished the 2002 season 17-15. It was our first winning season, and we finished fourth in the WNBA. I shot over 50 percent from the field and was named all-time leader in rebounds and games played at 93 minutes. I was second in Storm history in points scored. But in our first-ever playoff game, the Storm couldn't overcome the hot-shooting Los Angeles Sparks and lost game one, 78-61.

In May 2003, Coach Dunn resigned from her position as the Storm's head coach, leaving a strong foundation to build upon. As a result, Anne "Coach D" Donovan from the Charlotte Sting was hired as the second head coach of the Seattle Storm. She added two assistant coaches, Jenny Boucek and Jessie Kenlaw. Coach D was a former basketball star, who had been inducted into the Women's Basketball Hall of Fame. She was a post player coach, so I was eager to learn from her. Although she was a no-nonsense coach, I discovered that she had a big heart inside her intimidating, six-foot-eight frame once I got to know her beyond her tough outer shell.

Training camp with Coach D was just as competitive and demanding as with Coach Dunn, but thankfully practices were much shorter. Coach D formed an all-male practice squad consisting of former Pac-10 players and former overseas players to practice against the Storm on a regular basis to assist with drills. I was accustomed to playing with male players, so I welcomed the challenge playing against good athletes with size, strength and quickness.

This season, Kamila and I were the only two original players left from the 2000 inaugural team, adding five-foot-seven Australian guards Tully Bevilaqua and Sandra Brondello, five-foot-ten forward Stacey Thomas, and six-foot-three center Alisa Burras. My favorite of the new players was the first-round eighth overall pick, six-foot-one center Jung Sun-Min, the first Korean WNBA player. Jung's English was just as ineffective as my Korean, so she had an interpreter trailing her at the Storm practices and games. I pushed to get acquainted with Jung due to my fascination of learning about different cultures, and the fact that she was the best player ever in the history of Korean women's basketball. The extent of our audible conversation consisted of her smiling, shaking her head yes or no, or staring at her interpreter in curiosity to translate what I was saying. I must admit the interpreter occasionally needed an interpreter when my Jamaican patois slipped out. As a foreign player, I knew how lonely it felt adjusting to a different country and culture.

During one game, Jung became frustrated for being called out of the game by Coach D and was benched next to me. Her eyes were teary, and mine were, too, but I was just hungry. I asked her interpreter, who stood behind the bench, to translate to her, "I am going to order us a pizza and chicken wings after the game," which was her favorite meal. The interpreter laughed and so did Jung, who then requested an extra-large pepperoni pizza and an order of 20 hot wings. I knew all too well that it wasn't easy changing your role as a player. In Korea, she was a star, and in the WNBA, mostly a bench player, which was similar to my life playing overseas. The difficulty of learning to adjust to a lesser role while still maintaining your dignity and focus was humbling. I encouraged Jung to savor the experience of being part of the most elite women's basketball league in the world, as I did. We all were basketball stars somewhere at some point, but roles did change once you hit the WNBA. Due to language barriers, we couldn't understand each other on the court, but we both understood the universal basketball language.

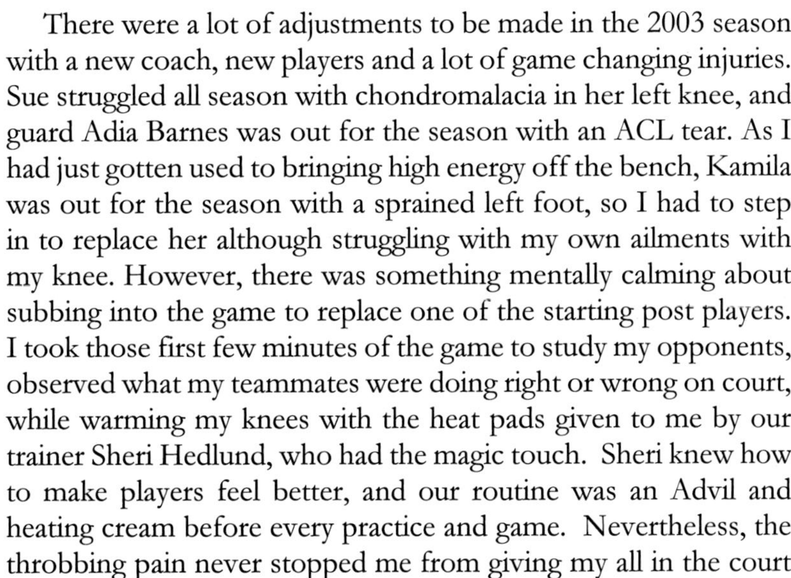

There were a lot of adjustments to be made in the 2003 season with a new coach, new players and a lot of game changing injuries. Sue struggled all season with chondromalacia in her left knee, and guard Adia Barnes was out for the season with an ACL tear. As I had just gotten used to bringing high energy off the bench, Kamila was out for the season with a sprained left foot, so I had to step in to replace her although struggling with my own ailments with my knee. However, there was something mentally calming about subbing into the game to replace one of the starting post players. I took those first few minutes of the game to study my opponents, observed what my teammates were doing right or wrong on court, while warming my knees with the heat pads given to me by our trainer Sheri Hedlund, who had the magic touch. Sheri knew how to make players feel better, and our routine was an Advil and heating cream before every practice and game. Nevertheless, the throbbing pain never stopped me from giving my all in the court because once I hit the court and the fans start cheering, I got an adrenalin rush and I felt nothing but excitement.

It was a disappointing season not making the playoffs but I was still optimistic about the next season. I knew each year I had to face the possibility of getting waived or traded but I was determined to hold on as long as I could until I got the Storm fans a championship. As an inaugural player, from the beginning our fans had shown me nothing but love. I was used to jumping over hurdles and facing the uncertain future, but I always prevailed through perseverance.

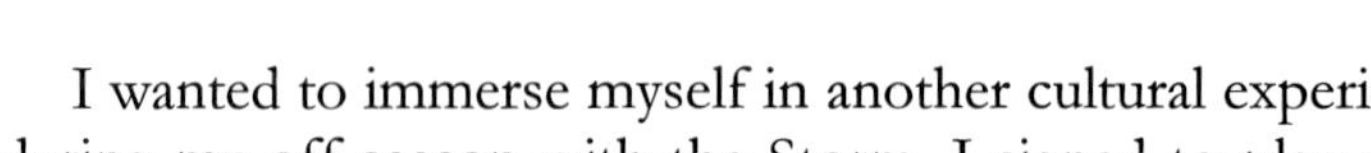

I wanted to immerse myself in another cultural experience, so during my off-season with the Storm, I signed to play with the Centro Energia team in Caserta, Italy in October 2003. Caserta was a small city that was so enchanting, where history greeted people on every corner with medieval villages, cathedrals, Roman architecture and a royal palace with the most beautiful English Garden. My new residence, Hotel Serenella was a boutique hotel with cozy vintage suites.

I befriended my Serbian teammate, six-foot-three guard Violeta "Vicki" Knezevic, who was fluent in five different languages, including Italian and English. I decided Vicki would teach me Italian but forgot to let her know, so I just kept asking her to translate.

My head coach was Massimo Riga whose English wasn't that good, so our assistant coach, Massimiliano "Maxi" Palmisani was his interpreter. Coach Riga signed me to ensure that the team advanced to the first division. I felt a bit pressured, but this situation was not all that unfamiliar to me because, for the past few years, I had similarly been recruited overseas to help teams improve their records.

For the duration of my contract, the team gave me a car but it was a stick-shift. I learned how to drive a stick-shift while in Iowa but had forgotten how to in the intervening years. Now, here I was in this compact European stick-shift car, all by myself, trying to reteach myself how to drive it. I drove pretty well, only stalling about 100 times on the way to practice, which was only five minutes from my hotel residence. Consequently, the commute took me about thirty minutes. However, I kept improving each day, getting to where I only stalled 95 times on the way to practice.

One day, I decided to go to the oceanside to immerse myself in the culture. I hopped in the car and started driving up a hill to see where it would lead me. When I stopped behind traffic going up this winding hill, I could not start the car again without rolling back. I started panicking. The cars behind me were honking as the traffic in front of me moved forward and got further and further away. I was totally out of my league driving a stick-shift, and of all places up a hill. Continuing to try and make it work, I rolled back and gently hit the car behind me. When I tried to move forward again with my car resting against his bumper, he started angrily honking his horn even more. I just turned the car off, exited and walked toward his car to apologize. After he saw my intimidating tall frame nearing him, his anger mysteriously disappeared. Though seemingly not being able to speak English, he said, "nessun problema," which translates "no problem" and quickly reversed his car and drove around me. After about 20 more cars drove around me, I had space to roll back, burned some rubber, and finally got the car to move forward. I made a conscious decision to not drive up anymore hilly roads. The only problem with my strategy to avoid hills, was that Caserta had an abundance of them.

The next day I told my assistant coach, Maxi, about my uphill adventure, and after he stopped crying from uncontrollable laughter, he offered to teach me how to properly drive a stick-shift uphill. With his driving lessons, I didn't roll backward much. That first experience however, scared me so I still tried to only drive the hills when there was little to no traffic.

A few weeks later, mommy flew in to visit with me. I took her to the Royal Palace of Caserta to tour the world's largest royal palace and the expansive English Garden that surrounded it. One of the most captivating corners of the English Garden was a fountain that fed a beautiful lake, the Bath of Venus which depicted the goddess' marble statue. Afterwards, mommy wanted to visit Rome, which was about two hours from Caserta. We traveled to Rome, taking in the Colosseum, an iconic ancient Roman gladiator arena and the site of many bloody fights. While walking inside the Colosseum, my imagination took me to another time. The next tour stop was

Vatican City, the temporal seat of the Pope. An independent state, entirely surrounded by the city of Rome, thousands of tourists visit each year to soak in its great history.

I enjoyed having mommy share in the abundance of my life, and I deeply appreciated her Jamaican cooking. It felt so good being able to show her that all of the sacrifices she made for me and my brothers as a single mother were not in vain.

My agents, Oded and Mike, told me that a few coaches had doubted that I could produce the same record in Italy that I had performed in Israel since they felt Italy had a stronger league. Though the Italian league was probably stronger, during the 2003 season in Italy, I hailed No. 1 in rebounds in the league and was one of the top five in scoring, erasing the doubts of those who questioned my ability to succeed outside of the Israeli league.

It still boggled my mind that I was a star player overseas, yet while playing in the WNBA, I wasn't. It was a difficult pill to swallow as my role changed each time I returned to the WNBA. I wanted to be the same player I was overseas, leading my team in points and rebounds, but it never happened. I played nearly forty minutes per game overseas, and only played half that time in the WNBA. Because of the amount of star players on the Storm team, they didn't require me to play as many minutes. I was a leader on court overseas and a role player in Seattle. In both instances, I played my role well. Though, in Seattle I longed to give more. It didn't matter how talented a player was, if they weren't given the opportunity to perform and showcase their skills.

In May 2004, I returned to Seattle, burned-out but motivated. I was uncertain if my body could go through the rigorous WNBA season, but I somehow found new energy. It was tough losing teammates I had grown attached to in previous seasons. But that became the norm. The Storm lost our starting shooting guard Sandy Brondello and Jung Sun-Min to the 2004 Olympics. Both players chose to remain in their home countries to play on their Olympic teams.

Nonetheless, I was curious to find out which new additions made the team. This season, the new players were mostly veterans who had played on other teams in the WNBA. They included five-foot-eight shooting guard Betty Lennox, five-foot-eleven small forward Sheri Sam, six-foot-five center Janelle Burse, six-foot-one forward Alicia Thompson, five-foot-nine guard Michelle Greco, and six-foot-two rookie Trina Frierson.

This season's team was so deep in talent, yet we found ourselves losing games we shouldn't have been losing. It seemed as if the coaching staff was blaming the substitute players who sat on the bench for the lack of productivity. The substitute players were understandably offended, so we called for a meeting between the players and the coaches. We expressed that we couldn't produce for the team if we weren't being used often. We reiterated to Coach D that it was unfair to let the starters work through their mistakes on court and not the bench players, yet expecting the same results. We couldn't give our best if we were pulled out after one mistake while trying to get into a groove. She listened, she heard and she adjusted.

My normal routine before games, was to lift weights, then head to the locker room to put on my jersey to prepare for the game. One particular game, however, I rushed back to the locker room for our game briefing and quickly put on my shooting shirt. One of the players got fouled, so Coach D put me in the game. I ran to the scoring table, and started pulling off my shooting shirt. As I lifted my shirt over my head, I only had on my bra. The referee standing in front of me was waving for me to come in, then paused in shock. My eyes and mouth were open wide in disbelief. I pulled my shooting shirt back down immediately, catching the attention of thousands in the crowd, who roared with laughter. I embarrassingly, hustled off the court to the locker room, while trying not to make eye contact with Coach D. As I passed the bench, my teammates were all dying with laughter, not even trying to hide their amusement at my expense. When I returned to the bench, Coach D called me once more to play in the game, grinning as I walked past her. After the game, I shared a good laugh in the locker room with my fellow teammates and coaches, and understandably so, my teammates never let me hear the last of that flashing incident.

In Coach D's first year, Lauren won the WNBA Most Valuable Player Award, but the team missed the playoffs, despite boasting the second-best scoring differential in the WNBA and with Sue injured for much of the year. Furthermore, the Storm finished the season with an 18-16 record, the most wins in franchise history.

Things got better in the regular season. The Storm pulled out a critical 65-63 victory against the Sacramento Monarchs on Betty Lennox's score with less than a second left in the game. Betty had always been a scorer, didn't fear anyone on court and wasn't afraid to take tough shots. The win helped propel the Storm to a season-high, six-game winning streak, including a sweep of a three-game road trip for the first time in Storm history.

The Storm team advanced for the second seed in the Western Conference Finals for playoffs after a 76-70 win at Indiana, and a 73-58 win over the Mercury. I knew that whenever my time on the court came, I would go hard and do whatever it took to help my team win. The Storm came out hot in Game 1, leading Sacramento 38-27 at the half, but the shooting inevitably cooled down as the Monarchs tightened their defense. After neither team could convert toward the end, the game headed to overtime. In the final seconds, the Monarchs defeated the Storm, 68-64.

The playoffs returned to Seattle with no room for error in Game 2. The Storm dominated most of the night, with a 66-54 win. In Game 3, the Storm was dominating the game, using a 20-0 second-half run to beat Sacramento 82-62 in the Western Conference Finals, winning our first Western Conference Championship. For the first time in franchise history, the Storm was in the WNBA Finals. The Final's structure was the best of three games against the Eastern Conference Finals victor, the Connecticut Sun.

Our first game was in Connecticut because we had home-court advantage due to our better win-loss record. Home-court advantage meant that two of the three games were going to be played on our home court, if there was a need for a third concluding game. Connecticut beat us 68-64 in a hard-fought first game. It was a tough loss, but we were confident since we were heading back to Seattle for the next two games. Fortunately, a sellout crowd of more than 17,000 fans was behind the Storm in Game 2. With home-court advantage, we got off to a quick start, but Connecticut caught up. However, Betty scored 16 of her 27 points after halftime. The game was a clear indication that Connecticut was not backing down, and they came to fight us for the championship. Connecticut got an open look at the buzzer on their final possession, but the shot hit the side of the backboard, and the Storm escaped with a 67-65 victory to force a third game.

Game 3, the final game of the season, the championship game, was on October 12, 2004. For me, this game was for all the young girls in Jamaica who thought that their dreams were unattainable because they were poor. This game was for the young girls all across the world who had been bullied for whatever reason, who had been thinking of giving up on working hard because they could not see immediate results. For me, this game was for the young girls who were afraid to try the impossible because too many voices around them had said what she dreamed couldn't be done. I so badly wanted this win, not just for me, my teammates, the fans, and the team owners, but for all the young girls out there who dared to be different.

As I looked at my teammates' faces before the game, I saw confidence, togetherness, and victory. We had become a strong team on and off the court. We put aside our individual goals for this one collective goal. Whether it was one minute in the game or 40 minutes, each player had to give it her all because it would take all of us to win this game.

The final game was intense. I did my part both on and off the court. My time on the court was spent diving after balls and putting up as many rebounds as possible. While on the bench, I was shouting, motivating the crowd into the game. The crowd and game were both electrifying. The game was intensely nerve-wracking, as Connecticut would not back down. Whenever my name was called, I hustled onto the court and gave it my all. In the final minutes of the game, I realized my ultimate professional dream was about to happen. The Storm had shut Connecticut down defensively, holding them without a score for more than 4 ½ minutes. The Storm fans were on their feet counting down the final seconds. As our opponents dribbled out the clock, the Seattle Storm defeated the Connecticut

Sun, 74-60. Our devoted Storm fans wildly cheered as the buzzer sounded, with confetti pouring from the ceiling and *Rock and Roll, Part Two* blaring in the arena. The Storm emerged victorious, winning the series 2–1. In the WNBA Finals, the Storm finished the season as champions with tears flowing in the stands and on the court.

Players rushed the court jumping, screaming and hugging each other before eventually finding the podium for the post-game ceremonies. Betty Lennox was deservingly named MVP of the Finals, and this championship was the best gift to our ever-faithful Seattle Storm fans. The win made Coach D the first female head coach in WNBA history to win the WNBA Championship, and this was Seattle's first national championship in 25 years in any sport – men's or women's. More importantly, the whole team contributed significantly, showing that all of our talents were valuable. The Storm staff quickly handed us our championship hats and shirts, as we took turns lifting the championship trophy. We cut the nets off the rim, and I felt as if I was inside a beautiful dream. But I was living my dream. I relished the role that I had, being the designated player who performed a freestyle Jamaican song right before the games to hype up the team and my infamous "shimmy shake" with Doppler, both of which became Storm traditions. I felt a deep sense of pride to know that I was part of the Seattle Storm story for every one of our games since the inaugural season.

This was it. The Seattle Storm were the 2004 WNBA champions. I was a WNBA champion. As the saying goes, "Good, better, best. Never let it rest. Until your good is better and your better is best."

CHAPTER 14

ONCE A CHAMPION, ALWAYS A CHAMPION

While savoring the moment of proudly hoisting the WNBA championship trophy over my head after the WNBA Finals, I felt as if everything in my life had come together. All the bullying I'd endured for being tall, all the sacrifices I'd made when I was training for basketball in Kingston, perfecting the fundamentals, all the pain and setbacks, the figures of authority with their own agendas of control. All of that I had contributed to the creation of this moment. I couldn't even feel my aching knees because of my adrenaline.

Yet somehow, I was deeply aware that my time in the WNBA was coming to an end. Despite the strain on my weakening knees, I practiced hard. Even when my knees were swollen and throbbing, I wanted to do whatever was required of me, giving the Storm all that I had both on and off the court.

Still on a championship high with the Storm, I went to Taranto, Italy, to play for a new team, Levoni Taranto. The coast of Taranto boasted beautiful natural landscapes with sheer cliffs and long stretches of sandy beaches that blended with the deep blue sea.

One of my teammates, six-foot-one forward Vicki Hall, used to play in the WNBA, so there was a familiar face on the team and a talented player who made the team stronger. Vicki was one of the toughest players I had ever played with or against as she hustled like the Energizer Bunny.

We advanced to the playoffs based on our position in the league. In a game preceding the playoffs, I landed directly on an opposing player's foot while she was guarding me on a jump shot. My right ankle forcefully twisted inward and I heard a loud pop. I hopped over to the bench enduring the stabbing pain. My ankle had swollen to the size of a grapefruit within minutes. Trainers used the overseas go-to ice spray on it, but it only worsened. I was rushed to the hospital after the game, and the doctor put a cast on my swollen ankle. Having had a few sprained ankles throughout my career, I knew I shouldn't have let him place a hard cast on it before the swelling went down. Still, I followed the doctor's orders. After a week, however, I demanded the removal of the cast. When the doctor removed it, my ankle was even more swollen and I couldn't walk on it. Psychologically, this battering of my body and spirit was deeply fatiguing to me.

I could no longer help my team, although the team manager offered to pay me an extra $10,000 to play in the playoffs. I worked hard to get the swelling down with ice and warm water, but to no avail. It was an extremely bad sprain, and the cast only weakened and worsened my ankle. All I could do now was to rehab and prepare for another WNBA season. Though, I didn't end my second Italian league season the way I anticipated, I was honored for community service work through my Simone4Children foundation and awarded The Women's Day Award in Italy from the International Women's Day Committee for being one of Jamaica's sports heroines. This was my first international honor, and I was extremely grateful for the recognition. I'd spent a lot of money and time on my foundation since its inception and made a promise to myself that I would get a community center built for the kids in my village in Kingston. After all that I had endured, no one could tell me there wasn't something or someone bigger than me orchestrating my life to get to that point. I was determined to keep my promise about getting the building built, as much as I was determined to make a difference in my country.

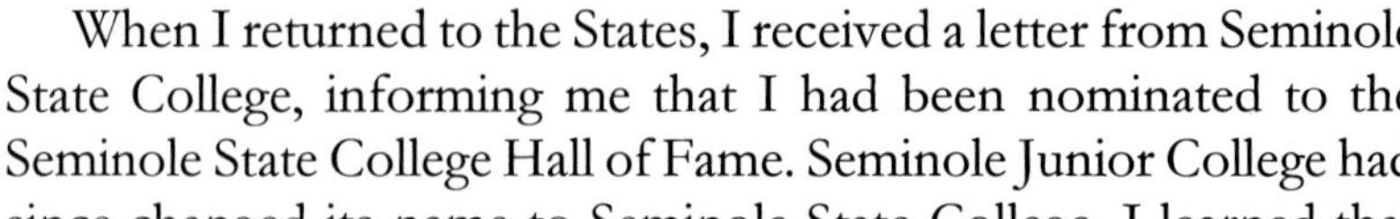

When I returned to the States, I received a letter from Seminole State College, informing me that I had been nominated to the Seminole State College Hall of Fame. Seminole Junior College had since changed its name to Seminole State College. I learned that

Coach Walck had nominated me, and said that it was a unanimous choice of the selection committee. I was deeply humbled to be inducted into the Hall of Fame from the school that started it all for my basketball career. As the first Black player, male or female, to receive this honor, I made every effort to attend this induction ceremony.

On May 5, 2005, my brother Gary, mommy, and Professor Chaffee all came to Seminole State College's Educational Foundation Recognition Banquet with over 350 in attendance to support me by witnessing my induction. Coach Walck introduced me, and began his speech saying, "The first time our athletic director, Dr. Thurman Edwards saw Simone Edwards work out, he told me that he did not think a better female athlete had ever been on campus." Coach Walck then revealed a secret he had held onto for more than 10 years, "When Simone was 17 years old, I spent several days going to her school at Kingston Technical High School to get all the necessary academic records required by the NJCAA. I was quite surprised when the principal was uncooperative in assisting with the process of gathering Simone's academic records. The principal expressed that she did not understand why I was recruiting Simone and not recruiting the school's top academic students. She actively encouraged me not to offer Simone a scholarship and said Simone would not be able to make the transition to an American college. Obviously, she was wrong." The attendees cheered in applause. Coach Walck went on to say, "I wasn't influenced by the principal's demands and stood by my confidence in Simone. I told the principal that I wanted to offer the scholarship to Simone Edwards, the player I was there for."

Sitting there and listening to Coach Walck share that story was disappointing and shocking to hear. I had never known that. It was a story that scratched at a scar. Someone comes to offer me a hand up, a way out of poverty, and now Coach Walck revealed that my principal, of all people, tried to block my scholarship opportunity by trying to convince him that someone else was more deserving than me. There it was again, so clearly, with the rock lifted up, exposing the broken, masked people hiding below. Figures of authority attempting to prevent me from achieving the things that I could have, the things that I might have. Right before I walked up to accept my award, I smirked, thinking to myself that the principal, like so many others along the way, certainly didn't have the last say when it came to my future.

It was May 2005. Since we had earned a WNBA championship title, I was now looking forward to visiting the White House to be honored by President George W. Bush, a celebratory ceremony in which all championship teams partake. When I arrived at training camp, I realized that our White House visit wasn't going to happen. I wasn't sure why it didn't happen, but I was incredibly disappointed that the Seattle Storm 2004 WNBA championship team weren't honored at the White House.

Much to my dismay, the Storm lost three of its marquee players with Kamila Vodičková, Tully Bevilaqua and Sheri Sam moving on to other teams. With Kamila traded to a new team, I now remained the only original player on the Storm roster. I took great pride in knowing that I had contributed to the Storm championship. The Storm opened the season against the Los Angeles Sparks. Before the game, the Storm had yet another shining moment as WNBA President Donna Orender presented players and coaches with our championship rings. This accomplishment cemented my name in the history books. It was the feeling of ultimate victory. After a magical season, the ring exemplified determination and pride.

When I finally had a chance to meet Donna Orender, I was taken aback that she was so approachable and down to earth. I talked with her about my foundation and its mission of helping children in Jamaica accumulate the skills and tools needed to help them realize their dreams. To my surprise, Donna then offered to donate $1,500 to my foundation. I was grateful for her generosity, and immediately used the funds to purchase groceries for 50 poor families in Kingston and covered expenses to send needy children to school. However, her generous financial contribution on behalf of the WNBA was only the tip of the iceberg.

Weeks later, Donna was traveling on a plane, seated next to a priest named Father Tony Palazzolo of Food for the Poor. She struck up a conversation with him, and he shared with her that he did missionary work in Jamaica. She remembered our brief conversation and proceeded to mention my work in Jamaica with children. After her flight, she called me to connect me to Father Tony. I felt so honored to know that she thought that much of the foundation's work to share that story and my work with someone else she had met who was similarly working on issues confronting the poor children of Jamaica.

I immediately called my friend, Jill Gallagher, a die-hard Storm fan and season ticket holder. Jill and her husband Bill sat behind the Storm bench every single game, which is how I came to know them. She later came on board as vice president of Simone4Children. Jill worked relentlessly for Simone4Children, including taking a flight to Kingston to provide school supplies, deliver groceries to needy families and assist in fundraising efforts.

I followed up with Father Tony, and he immediately arranged a meeting in a South Florida office with Mr. Robin Mahfood, president and CEO of Food for the Poor. I took a quick flight to Florida with no proposal, no brochures, no diagrams and one picture. One of our foundation program pillars covered education, and we were introduced to a program that was started by Dean Rhoden, a childhood friend of mine who had formed the first scout troop in the Hermitage neighborhood. I decided to work with Dean because of my respect for him and the work he was doing in the community.

There were students who attended the University of the West Indies and the University of Technology who volunteered their time to teach and tutor the students to help them with homework and exam preparation. In return, the university students received school credit for their time. Although the program was successful, the students were learning out of an old, empty, rusty school bus in which Dean had replaced the bus seats with old metal chairs. Everything, including the chairs and table, was broken and filled with rust.

I was so touched by the situation and felt the pull to help because these children cared more about their education than their inconvenience. They showed up each day to receive help, rain or shine. When I was given the opportunity to meet with Mr.

Mahfood, all I had to work with was one piece of paper that contained a picture of that old, rusty school bus.

I walked into Mr. Mahfood's office with that piece of paper, feeling a bit intimidated as I sat in front of him. He ran one of the largest nonprofit organizations in the world, and I had nothing to show except my heart, my vision, and a picture of the old, rusty school bus. I told him I made a promise to God that, if I got out of my deeply impoverished village, I would return and build a community center for the kids of Gola. I showed him the picture I was holding and said, "Coming from a small, rural village in Kingston, Jamaica, that did not share in the economic wealth some communities witness in the tourism zones on the island gave me a heart for similar people from tough backgrounds. It's a heart wanting to give back to my community in appreciation for my success that made it possible for me to leave my small village and its over-abundance of economic challenges." I didn't know what else to say. This was very new to me, to be requesting aid from someone who could really help a lot if our efforts matched his efforts.

He responded, "I can see your passion Simone, so I am going to help you fulfill your promise. I will donate a building." I was flabbergasted, uncertain what had just happened. A building? All I was expecting was some school supplies, tables and chairs, and Mr. Mahfood had just offered me a building. I didn't move because I knew I'd jump right out the chair and leap towards the ceiling in my celebration of what had just happened. Instead, I just sat there, stunned, fighting to hold back the tears and screams of absolute joy and gratitude. I wanted to hug and kiss him or even give him a high-five, but I settled for a handshake. I graciously thanked him and floated out of his office on cloud nine.

I called Father Tony and Donna to personally thank them. They both were gracious and humble in sharing in my enthusiasm. Donna then disclosed to me that Seattle was her first stop upon becoming president of the WNBA and that I was the first-ever WNBA player she met and talked to personally. Donna genuinely wanted to know more about me, not only as a player, but as a person. I shared my dream with her to help others, which she helped turn into a reality beyond my expectations.

The portable brick building was placed in Hermitage. The building donated by Food for the Poor had two classrooms, two chalkboards, new tables and chairs, one kitchen with a fridge and stove, and an office. The Hermitage and Gola community were deeply grateful. It was another pinnacle moment of joy and pride. I had fulfilled my promise to myself to give back and support children's lives through my foundation.

After the 2005 Storm season, I went to a new team, Halcon Avenida, in Salamanca, Spain, an ancient university town situated in the west of Spain. One of my teammates, six-foot-four power forward Kelly Schumacher, also played in the WNBA. She wore her long blonde hair in a braid and was a dominant inside player like myself. However, my knees were so worn out by then that I had a hard time warming up before the games. I'd played year-round since 2000, and all that pounding from jumping and sprinting and quick stopping was taking a toll on my body. I was tired, but basketball defined so much of my life. I pushed myself as we advanced to the playoffs, winning the Spanish Copa de la Reina championship. My knees had had enough, and though my heart and mind wanted to be a professional athlete forever, my knee suggested otherwise.

I returned to the Seattle in May 2006, knowing this would probably be my last season with the WNBA. Throughout six years with the Storm, I had watched many new teammates come and many teammates who had become friends, traded or waived. I had experienced from only six wins in a season to winning a WNBA championship. I had watched infants who could barely roll over on their sides grow into grade-school children, running across the court to ask for autographs before or after a game.

But my knees had run their course, and it now took me 10 minutes to do pre-warms before my warm-ups. It was time. This realization tore my heart into pieces. The reality of it all was that I could no longer play at the level I truly wanted to play, and there were younger players out there who were looking to get into the WNBA. They certainly deserved their shot. I had mine. It was no easy feat to enter the WNBA or even remain, and in my dream of dreams, I had not only made it into this elite club, but I had stayed in and won a championship. I was so proud that I had been part of such a great organization over these inaugural years. The strong sense of family and professionalism that was exuded by the Storm organization was a fabric of my life.

It was with a wince of emotional pain during pre-season when Coach D stopped by my residence to speak about the future that had come too soon. It was so emotional for both of us that day in my Seattle home. We spoke about my time with the Storm and my declining knee strength. She told me the Storm wanted to honor my retirement on the court in front of all the fans. I was the only original member who had played in the Seattle Storm uniform since 2000.

The Storm's farewell sendoff was emotional for me, the coaches, players, and fans. Karen Bryant, the Storm's chief operating officer was teary-eyed as she shared her goodbyes. She had always treated benchwarmers the same as she treated our marquee stars. Karen expressed that I was a very important part of the Storm organization, and it felt good knowing that.

My dream of playing basketball professionally had come to an end as I had reached unsurmountable goals while playing in the WNBA. Together with the organization, teammates, and fans, I officially retired on May 19, 2006 as the franchise's leader in games played, third in rebounds, and fourth in points. I entered the WNBA when I couldn't see the light at the end of the tunnel and came out stronger on the other side.

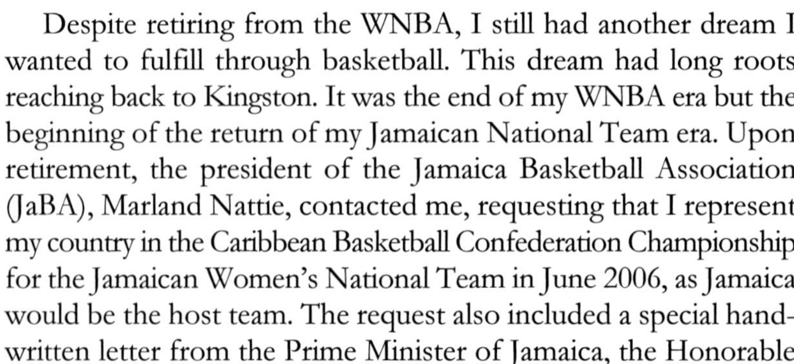

Despite retiring from the WNBA, I still had another dream I wanted to fulfill through basketball. This dream had long roots reaching back to Kingston. It was the end of my WNBA era but the beginning of the return of my Jamaican National Team era. Upon retirement, the president of the Jamaica Basketball Association (JaBA), Marland Nattie, contacted me, requesting that I represent my country in the Caribbean Basketball Confederation Championship for the Jamaican Women's National Team in June 2006, as Jamaica would be the host team. The request also included a special handwritten letter from the Prime Minister of Jamaica, the Honorable

Portia Simpson Miller. I felt national pride, honored and very humbled.

The timing was perfect because I hoped to play again in my home country. The last time I played in Jamaica, I was only a 16 year old benchwarmer, with Coach Walck scouting to see me play. Now, although I was no longer at the top of my game and hampered by old injuries, I was still good enough to make a difference during a short tournament.

The five-day tournament was scheduled in Kingston, June 13 - 17, 2006, and brought together five international Caribbean teams competing for the women's championship. National teams came from Antigua, Barbados, Virgin Islands, Bahamas, and Jamaica. I was eager to see friends and family, so I arrived a few days early for training.

The games were scheduled to occur in the new stadium that had been built in Kingston while I had been playing ball around the world. We trained inside of the same gym I had with the Mustangs Phillies' Coach Smiley 15 years earlier. Returning to Kingston, back here where it all began, I had come full circle. Now I was a starting player on the National Team, and the respect I hadn't yet earned back then, I was receiving at this moment.

Enid Angus was the vice president of overseas operations for JaBA, and was instrumental in putting the team together. Our high-energy team manager was Clofyeld "Patsy" Thomas who was well connected. The two of us had an introductory meeting with the Prime Minister of Jamaica, the Honorable Portia Simpson Miller. She thanked me for my participation with the Jamaican National Team and congratulated me on my successful professional basketball career. She seemed most genuine in offering that I made Jamaica proud.

On the day of the tournament, we headed to the locker room to discuss basketball strategies with our head coach Rerita Essanason, I realized that there was little she could tell us about any of the competing teams because she had no statistics on the players. On paper, we were the strongest team in the competition based on our basketball profiles, as our team consisted of local and overseas players – Oberon Pitterson, Vanessa Giddon, Shawnette Redley, Tamika Lemonius, Alecia Fung, Elfreda Reid, Sharon Wiles, Erika

Messam, Syreeta Rose, and Althea Byfield. Our greatest weakness was the small amount of time we had to practice together as a team in order to build on court chemistry.

I stared down at my uniform. I couldn't have felt prouder to represent my home country. I was home on Jamaican soil to represent my country for the second time. These were my Jamaican people, the people who shaped everything I had to drive me to compete and succeed. I walked inside of the stadium, I felt something I could never have felt at 16 years old. I felt tremendous confidence.

Out on the court, I looked around for my family, but no one was there. We went through warm-ups to prepare for the game. While preparing, I heard someone calling my name. Walking into the stadium were mommy, my brothers, sisters, nephews, nieces and Mama Nancy. Now, I was ready.

Soon the buzzer went off, and we went through our team introductions. My heart was racing. The announcer called my name, "Simone Edwards," and I heard my family and the crowd cheering with excitement. I waved to them and went to line up on the court for the national anthem. I stood teary-eyed, experiencing a flood of so many different emotions. So much came together for me in that moment, standing on that court, in that arena, among those people and wrapped so thoroughly in so many memories.

We shook hands with our first opponents, the U.S. Virgin Islands team. The buzzer went off for us to clear the court and do our last-minute prep work to get ready to start. From the first tipoff, we had that first game in our control. I wanted to dominate to fulfill my promise to myself when I was 16 – the promise that I'd return home to play for my country. I was seven for eight from the field, and I finished with 16 points. I chuckled as I finished our first game with the same number of points as the age I was when I first represented Jamaica. Sixteen. We won, 102-55.

The next few tournament games were just as brutal for the other teams. Our team won every game throughout the tournament, dominating each team as we advanced to the final game. This return to Jamaican basketball was so meaningful for me. I had to win a championship for my Jamaica. I had something to prove to myself. So, in our final game, we played against the Bahamas. They were double- and triple-teaming me, placing two or three players on me. The crowd got louder and louder as we moved closer to the end of the game. Mommy screamed so loud, she lost her voice. Patsy and Enid were going berserk, cheering like crazy. By now, our team had chemistry on the court, and I managed to score 15 points. The final buzzer went off, and the crowd was chanting "Jamaica," as our team started jumping and screaming. It felt so wonderful to watch loved ones, who had believed in me, experience this moment, cheering and screaming and beaming with exuberant Jamaican pride. The Jamaican Women's National Basketball team was the 2006 Caribbean Basketball Confederation Champions, winning 90-46 against the Bahamas and claiming the title for our Jamaica.

I had departed Kingston with a dream and returned a welcomed and respected champion.

EPILOGUE

WALKING TO GREATNESS

As I look back on my childhood, I can only smile. My dream to not only visit America but also live there came true. America is so far-fetched a goal or dream for so many poor kids in the Caribbean that it becomes just a silly fantasy for many. Accidentally, with regards to something for which I neither planned nor prepared, the game of basketball gave me an opportunity to make my dreams a reality. I thought my speed in running was going to give me opportunity, but it turned out I had to learn to slow down and dribble to find my hope.

I recall every single time I could have quit, felt like I should, and almost did – and it boggles my mind that, somehow, I never did. From being bullied, to practicing barefoot in the scorching sun, to wearing my mom's oversized shoes to school, to walking miles, not by choice but by circumstances. So many things worked against my achieving any sort of dream or success. As I was taunted, I didn't quit striving because I wanted to shine as bright as the stars that lit up my village at night. I didn't quit because my role models, mommy and Mama Nancy, made so many sacrifices for me. I didn't quit when my father ran beside me on the sidelines, encouraging me to not slow down. I didn't quit because of earth angels supporting and pushing me so much so that I got more and more comfortable with creating my own way when my first attempts on a path were blocked.

Being poor meant that I had less access to many resources that help most people succeed, but it didn't mean that I lacked dreams, ambition, strength, endurance, tolerance or resilience. Because I had an abundance of those characteristics, I was able to realize that my current circumstances did not dictate my future.

I just wasn't willing to settle for less than what I wanted. I couldn't find valid excuses to satisfy myself, no matter how many I conjured up. I didn't give up because I somehow always found a way to believe in my capabilities even in the midst of my greatest self-doubt.

To be honest, it really wasn't about something in me that made success possible. Sometimes, life aligns itself in such a way that the cost of failure is so high and so frightening, that there is nothing to do but try again. Fear of failing what others believe you are capable of is exceedingly motivating.

I didn't always know what to believe, but people who loved me believed in me. That so often became enough to make me struggle and fight just a little more. My struggles seemed so unbearable at times. Yet I reached the other side of the struggle and found that I could bear more than I ever thought I could. My hunger for success always seemed to be just a little bit stronger, than that of others. With each success at facing the darkness, the hunger got stronger. If I was going to fail, it wouldn't be because I didn't try. In the end, failing wasn't an option for me. Most of the time, you don't know when you're winning in battle until you've won.

I became a champion for all the girls and boys seemingly locked in poverty who had lost hope of ever achieving success because of their present situation. I want them to have a story. I want them to learn and be energized to know that each challenge in their lives is only temporary – but only if you make it so. Success is not for those who overly doubt themselves but for those who believe in themselves and are willing to work hard to accomplish their goals. I want them to be proud of who they are and where they come from.

Despite all the cheers and awards and accolades, I was always connected to my country, Jamaica. Always in the back of my head was my Gola village, with all of its grinding poverty and violence, shaping the dreams of its children who had yet to find a way free of that poverty.

A day doesn't go by that I don't think about my beautiful country, the way the sun sets, its beautiful beaches, and the stars that light up the sky at night. Being able to move to America and being provided an education and professional sports career was life changing. It compelled me to work even harder to ensure more children who shared a similar background with me are able to participate in finding and building greater opportunity as well.

To build that part of my dream, the "give-back dream," it was necessary for me to be hyper-focused, through every obstacle. I recognized that the opportunities provided to me in America afforded me some real economic opportunity that I would have never had if Coach Gary Hudson and Coach Smiley had never spotted me at the track meet. I am deeply aware of how blessed I have been. Every opportunity and difficulty combined to put me on this platform to make a difference in children's lives. Despite every obstacle, I kept my eyes on the prize. Each day of my childhood as I walked the dusty roads of Gola, I dreamed in my heart that I was walking to greatness. I refused to be broken. I was determined to be unstoppable.

ACKNOWLEDGMENTS

I departed Kingston, Jamaica with a dream and returned home a champion. I want to thank God for giving me the chance to share my life experiences on and off the basketball court through these chapters. Thanks to my mommy Beryl Edwards, my daddy Aston Edwards, my mama Nancy Coley, and all my family for supporting me during my college and professional basketball careers and beyond. Thanks to all the coaches who believed in me – Coach Keith "Smiley" Daily, Coach Marland Nattie, Coach Gary Hudson, Coach Brad Walck, Coach C. Vivian Stringer, Coach Nancy Darsch, Coach Linn Dunn, Coach Ann Donovan, Coach Eli Rabi, Coach Rose Peeples, Coach Rerita Essanason and Coach Tim Eatman. And to my trainers, Roxann Dahl, Deborah Corbatto, Sheri Hedlund and Karen Parker for strengthening my knees and spirit.

For your continued support, true friendship, and commitment to Simone4Children Foundation and The Anti-Bully Project, my heartfelt thanks to Clofyeld "Patsy" Thomas, Enid Angus, Jill Gallagher, Kiesha Lindsay, as well as to Food For The Poor for donating a building to Simone4Children to continue to help make positive changes in children's lives.

Thanks to my mentor, Mark Chaffee, for your friendship and assistance with book editing.

Special appreciation to Rob "Waldo" Waldman and Courtney McFarlane for your great encouragement. And my deepest gratitude to The Hon. Dr. Geneive Brown Metzger, Donna Orender, and to Manuela and James Goren for your continuous support and friendship beyond description.

I am grateful to St. Francis All-Age School, Kingston Technical High School, Mustangs Phillies, Seminole State College, Amateur Athletic Union (AAU), University of Iowa, Women's National

Basketball Association (WNBA), New York Liberty, Seattle Storm, and the Jamaica Women's National Team for helping me lay the groundwork for personal and professional success.

A special acknowledgment of gratitude to my GoFundMe contributors for being part of this invaluable project: Deborah Corbatto, Marianne Simonton, Brad Walck, Shelly Henry-Sharp, Jessica McKimmie, Demoya Williams, Sarah Lauer, Aggie Clark, Shaina Rosario, Father Anthony Palazzolo, Sean Lee, Antonio d'Albero, Lee Haworth, Cheri Webb, Conrad Cook, Hannah Phillips, Anne Donovan, and Rose Peeples. I am humbled and thankful.

Heartfelt thanks to my co-writer, Jobi Tyson for walking through this journey with me. You were able to capture and put together the essence of I who was and who I became throughout this book. You are deeply appreciated.

Saying that life for me has had its share of obstacles, would be an understatement. Thank you to all who believed in me. For those who didn't and caused me hurt, shame, or pain, I must say to you that your negative energy was lost on me because I became stronger and more resilient.

All my love to children and teens experiencing bullying – love yourself, keep going and keep smiling.

Tuh mi Jamaican peeps. Big up yuself. One luv!

SIMONE EDWARDS

There's something magical about the ability to transform unbearable circumstances into beautiful scenes that reveal a deeper truth. Sincerest thanks to the following, whose interviews enriched *Unstoppable*:

Beryl Edwards, Aston Edwards, Brad Walck, Keith "Smiley" Daily, Mark Chaffee, Nancy Darsch, Donna Orender, Anne Donovan, C. Vivian Stringer, Margaret Alston, Teresa Weatherspoon, Jasmina Perazic-Gipe, Nadine Domond, Enid Angus, Clofyeld "Patsy" Thomas, Juddeth Edwards, and Venece Edwards.

I appreciate the trust, cooperation, and friendship of Simone Edwards. Thanks for your graciousness and openness throughout this cathartic book-writing process. Your confidence in me as a writer and confidante for a project that's been hatching for more than a decade has been life changing. From the beginning, the goal of this memoir was to capture the origins of Simone's resilience in the face of opposition to the rise of a champion, allowing her story and legacy to unfold through her eyes and voice. Our long talks in Kingston, Jamaica at her childhood home and surrounding areas were our most fruitful, which is no surprise since Simone's roots run deepest there.

Candice Davis, our structural editor of Go Write Something, was a long-time believer in Simone's story from the start – I am grateful and potentially wiser because of your guidance. Special gratitude to our copy editor, Mark Chaffee, for your devotion to clearing the truest path into the heart and guts of each tale, which was instrumental in shaping the final narrative. For going above and beyond with beta reading, heartfelt thanks to my college friend Laquanta Sandifer, and special thanks to Paula Chaffee Scardamalia for your invaluable feedback and enthusiastic support, Pat Burson George for your boundless knowledge in the final editing, and Anita R. Henderson of The Write Image, LLC for your encouragement, continuous support, and for using your magic to proofread the book.

And, lastly, love to my family, and special gratitude to my first cousin and filmmaker Jonathan Bowens of Qloudy Sunshine for your support and documenting this consuming and fulfilling project.

Vision is seeing the invisible.

JOBI TYSON

ABOUT THE AUTHORS

Photo Credit: Tim Baldwin/Vibbin Photography

SIMONE EDWARDS is a WNBA champion who has inspired thousands with her upbeat and positive attitude in overcoming the obstacles put before her. The first Caribbean and first Jamaican to play in the WNBA was signed to the New York Liberty and Seattle Storm. She is a sports columnist and sought-after motivational speaker who travels the globe inspiring audiences with her story of resilience. She is also the founder of Simone4Children and its global movement, The Anti-Bully Project. She is a graduate of Seminole State College and the University of Iowa. She is a native of Kingston, Jamaica.

JOBI TYSON, MBA is a cultural researcher, writer, brand strategist and web series creator. She is the founder of Starstruck Ventures, a sports and entertainment career transition firm, specializing in helping people with public platforms tell their stories. She is also the managing partner of Diverse Writers Room, and a graduate of Bethune-Cookman University and the University of Phoenix. She is a native of Pompano Beach, Florida.